# SIMPLE
# PMP

---

## PMBOK Quiz

### Updated for the PMBOK
### Guide Sixth Edition

# Phil Martin

Contents

4

# How to Use This Book

This book has two types of material – questions and terms.

When you see this:

> *Question:*

You will be asked a question and you need to provide an answer – more often than not the answer is in the form of a bulleted list.

When you see this:

> *Define:*

You must provide the definition for the given term. Pretty simple.

This book's layout mirrors the companion *Simple PMP Exam Guide*. This was done on purpose to make it easy for you to locate more information on any subject you run across. Just go to that chapter in *Simple PMP Exam Guide* and look for the corresponding paragraph – it will be in the same order in which the questions and terms are presented in this book.

**Section 1** contains basic concepts to get you started.

**Section 2** introduces more advanced topics, and provides a lot of information on terms you will need to know.

**Section 3** dives into each knowledge area, and will quiz you on ITTOs. If you don't know what an ITTO is, STOP NOW: you are not ready for this book.

At then end are two additional resources:

- Common Acronyms, which gives you the acronym, and you must provide the term
- Definitions, which are terms and definitions, but word-for-word as they appear in the PMBOK Guide.

**An audio version of this print book is available on audible.com!**

# Section 1: Basic Concepts

**Processes**

Knowledge Area / Process Groups matrix:

| Process Groups | Project Integration Management | Project Scope Management | Project Schedule Management | Project Cost Management | Project Quality Management | Project Resource Management | Project Communications Management | Project Risk Management | Project Procurement Management | Project Stakeholder Management |
|---|---|---|---|---|---|---|---|---|---|---|
| Initiating | Develop Project Charter | | | | | | | | | Identify Stakeholders |
| Planning | Develop Project Management Plan | Plan Scope Management<br>Collect Requirements<br>Define Scope<br>Create WBS | Plan Schedule Management<br>Define Activities<br>Sequence Activities<br>Estimate Activity Duration<br>Develop Schedule | Plan Cost Management<br>Estimate Costs<br>Determine Budget | Plan Quality Management | Plan Resource Management<br>Estimate Activity Resources | Plan Communications Management | Plan Risk Management<br>Identify Risks<br>Perform Qualitative Risk Analysis<br>Perform Quantitative Risk Analysis<br>Plan Risk Responses | Plan Procurement Management | Plan Stakeholder Engagement |
| Executing | Direct and Manage Project Work<br>Manage Project Knowledge | | | | Manage Quality | Acquire Resources<br>Develop Team<br>Manage Team | Manage Communications | Implement Risk Responses | Conduct Procurements | Manage Stakeholder Engagement |
| Monitoring and Controlling | Monitor and Control Project Work<br>Perform Integrated Change Control | Validate Scope<br>Control Scope | Control Schedule | Control Costs | Control Quality | Control Resources | Monitor Communications | Monitor Risks | Control Procurements | Monitor Stakeholder Engagement |
| Closing | Close Project or Phase | | | | | | | | | |

# Chapter 1: Here's the Deal

*Define:* **Knowledge area**

A subject that represents one broad topic on project management.

*Question:* **How many knowledge areas are there?**

10

# Chapter 2: Agile Methodologies

*Question:* **What two needs does agile address?**

- Start executing the project in a safe manner before all requirements are known.
- React quickly and predictably to changing project conditions.

*Define:* **Sprint**

An iteration in Scrum.

*Define:* **User story**

Textual requirements to be delivered when using Scrum.

*Define:* **Backlog**

A prioritized list of user stories when using Scrum.

*Define:* **Time periods**

PMBOK's name for iterations or sprints.

*Define:* **Product owner**

A role in Scrum that decides what we're going to build and in what order.

*Define:* **Team**

A role in Scrum that decides how long it will take to build something and then does it.

*Define:* **Grooming**

A ceremony in Scrum where the Product Owner shows the team potential user stories, and they collaboratively add detail till both are satisfied.

*Define:* **Planning**

A ceremony in Scrum where the team commits to all the user stories it can complete in the upcoming sprint.

*Define:* **Daily Standups**

A ceremony in Scrum where everyone gathers once each morning to discuss what they did yesterday, what they are going to do today, and if they are being blocked by anything.

*Define:* **Review**

A ceremony in Scrum where the team shows the Product Owner what they have completed in the last sprint.

*Define:* **Retrospective**

A ceremony in Scrum where everyone discusses what went wrong and what went right in the previous sprint.

*Define:* **Story Point**

A unitless number representing the level of effort a given story will take to complete.

*Define:* **Velocity**

The number of story points a team can complete in one sprint.

# Chapter 3: Projects, Programs, Portfolios and Operations

*Define:* **Project**

A temporary effort to create something unique.

*Define:* **Business value**

The net quantifiable benefit derived from a business endeavor.

*Question:* **What are the 4 project initiation context categories?**

- To meet regulatory, legal or social requirements
- To satisfy stakeholder needs
- To implement or change strategies
- To create or make better products, processes or services

*Define:* **Factor**

A good reason to start a project.

*Define:* **Project management**

The application of knowledge, skills, tools and techniques to activities so that we can meet the project requirements.

*Define:* **Project**

Represents where the work is done.

*Define:* **Program**

Allows us to manage multiple projects (or even multiple programs) at once.

*Question:* **Of portfolio, program and project, which tells us how to reach our goal?**

Program and project.

*Question:* **Of portfolio, program and project, which tells us which goal we should be trying to reach?**

Portfolio.

*Define:* **Megaprojects**

Really large projects that typically cost more than $1 billion, impact more than 1 million people, and can go on for years.

*Define:* **Portfolio**

Contains two or more programs, portfolios and even individual projects.

*Question:* **What question does a portfolio answer?**

'Are we doing the right things?'

11

*Question:* **What question does a program or project answer?**

'Are we doing things the right way?'

---

*Define:* **Strategic objective**

The goal of a portfolio.

---

*Define:* **Operations management**

Makes sure that a business can efficiently use resources to churn out products or services as desired.

---

*Define:* **Organizational environment**

Comprised of an overarching strategy, portfolios, programs, projects and operations, along with all the interactions between those components.

---

*Define:* **Organizational project management, or OPM**

Manages the organizational environment.

---

*Question:* **What does OPM ensure?**

- …everyone understands what we're doing, why we're doing it and how we're going to get it done
- …the right projects are executed
- … resources are allocated properly

---

# Chapter 4: Project and Development Life Cycles

*Define:* **Project life cycle**

The series of steps of which every project is comprised.

*Question:* **What are the 5 types of project life cycles?**

- Predictive
- Iterative
- Incremental
- Adaptive
- Hybrid

*Define:* **Predictive life cycle**

An approach that requires everything to be defined up-front before work begins, and only produces value after complete.

*Define:* **Iterative life cycle**

An approach where we know most of the project scope before it starts, and each iteration produces something of value.

*Define:* **Incremental life cycle**

An approach similar to the iterative approach, but is time-boxed and produces no value until the end.

*Define:* **Adaptive life cycle**

An approach that is like the iterative life cycle, but the scope can change after each iteration. Can be agile, iterative or incremental.

*Define:* **Hybrid life cycle**

An approach that combines predictive and adaptive.

*Define:* **Product**

Something that is created by a project.

*Define:* **Phase**

A collection of activities that results in a deliverable of some type.

*Question:* **What are the 6 phase primary attributes?**

- Name
- Number
- Duration
- Resource requirements
- Entrance criteria
- Exit criteria

*Define:* **Resource requirements (phase attribute)**

Comprised of people, equipment or rooms.

*Define:* **Entrance criteria (phase attribute)**

The items required before a phase can start.

---

*Define:* **Exit criteria (phase attribute)**

The items that must be completed before a phase can end.

---

*Question:* **What are 2 reasons to use phases?**

- They provide better insight to managing the project
- They provide a natural checkpoint after each phase to course-correct before the next phase begins

---

*Define:* **Phase gate**

A checkpoint at the end of a phase to measure progress against the project's original documentation.

---

*Question:* **What are other names for a phase gate?**

A phase review, stage gate, or kill point.

---

*Question:* **What are the 5 options we can take when we reach a phase gate?**

- ...remain in the current phase
- ...repeat the current phase, or maybe just repeat some elements within the current phase
- ...continue to the next phase with modification
- ...continue to the next phase with no modifications
- ...end the project

---

*Define:* **Process**

Various activities that are executed at specific times within the project life cycle.

---

*Question:* **What are the two types of process outputs?**

- ...an input to another process, or
- ...a deliverable of the project or phase

---

*Question:* **What are the 3 ITTO sections?**

- ...inputs
- ...tools & techniques
- ...outputs

---

*Question:* **What are the 3 process categories?**

- ...used once or at predefined intervals
- ...performed as-needed
- ...performed continuously during the entire project

---

*Question:* **What are the 5 process groups?**

- Initiating process group
- Planning process group
- Executing process group
- Monitoring and controlling process group
- Closing process group

---

*Question:* **What is the purpose of the initiating process group?**

To define a new project or phase, get authorization to start it, and then begin.

---

*Question:* **What is the purpose of the planning process group?**

To establish scope and define goals.

---

*Question:* **What is the purpose of the executing process group?**

To do the actual work.

---

*Question:* **What is the purpose of the monitoring and controlling process group?**

To track how things are going and make changes as needed.

---

*Question:* **What is the purpose of the closing process group?**

To close out a project or phase

---

*Question:* **What are the 10 different knowledge areas, in order?**

- Integration
- Scope
- Schedule
- Cost
- Quality
- Resource
- Communications
- Risk
- Procurement
- Stakeholder

---

*Question:* **What is the purpose for the Project Integration Management knowledge area?**

To identify and coordinate other processes.

---

*Question:* **What is the purpose for the Project Scope Management knowledge area?**

To ensure the project stays true to the defined scope – not too little and not too much.

---

*Question:* **What is the purpose for the Project Schedule Management knowledge area?**

To make sure the project finishes on-time.

---

*Question:* **What is the purpose for the Project Cost Management knowledge area?**

To make sure the project stays within budget.

---

*Question:* **What is the purpose for the Project Quality Management knowledge area?**

To ensure the project creates what the stakeholder wanted.

---

*Question:* **What is the purpose for the Project Resource Management knowledge area?**

To ensure all required resources are available when needed.

---

*Question:* **What is the purpose for the Project Communications Management knowledge area?**

To make sure that all project information is created, shared, and disposed of properly.

---

*Question:* **What is the purpose for the Project Risk Management knowledge area?**

To identify and manage risk of failure.

---

*Question:* **What is the purpose for the Project Procurement Management knowledge area?**

To control the acquisition of anything needed from outside sources.

---

*Question:* **What is the purpose for the Project Stakeholder Management knowledge area?**

To identify all possible stakeholders, record their expectations, and ensure they remain engaged.

---

*Question:* **What are the 3 types of data that must be tracked?**

- Work performance data
- Work performance information
- Work performance reports

---

*Define:* **Work performance data**

All raw observations and measurements.

---

*Define:* **Work performance information**

The status of deliverables and change requests, along with estimates till we are done.

---

*Define:* **Work performance reports**

A collection of all reports – both physical and electronic – used to alert people about issues and force decisions to be made.

---

*Question:* **What are the 4 major business documents?**

- Business case
- Benefits management plan
- Project charter
- Project management plan

---

*Define:* **Business case**

A document that spells out the justification and goal for the project and is provided by the sponsor.

---

*Question:* **What are 7 reasons a business case is created?**

- Market demand
- Organizational need
- Customer request
- Technological advance
- Legal requirement
- Ecological impacts
- Social need

---

*Define:* **Benefits management plan**

A document describing the processes used to achieve the goals set in the Business Case.

*Define:* **Project charter**

A document created by the project sponsor, and authorizes a project along with the needed resources.

*Define:* **Project management plan**

A document describing how a project will be executed, monitored and controlled.

*Define:* **Needs assessment**

A document that examines a need and recommends what we do to meet that need.

*Question:* **What are the 4 major components of a business case?**

- Needs
- An analysis of the situation
- A recommendation
- An evaluation

*Question:* **What does the needs component of the business case provide?**

Why we are acting, the problem to be solved, stakeholders involved and project scope.

*Question:* **What does the analysis component of the business case provide?**

Existing strategies and goals, root cause, a gap analysis, risks, and possible solutions.

*Question:* **What does the recommendation component of the business case provide?**

The best solution, how it will be implemented, and how we will measure success of the project.

*Question:* **What does the evaluation component of the business case provide?**

How we will measure the benefits of the deliverable.

*Define:* **Benefits Management Plan**

A document stating when the project will end and how we will measure success.

*Question:* **What are the 6 items the benefits management plan includes?**

- Target benefits
- Strategic alignment
- Timeframe for realizing benefits
- Benefits owner
- Metrics
- Assumptions
- Risks

*Define:* **Target benefits (benefits management plan item)**

The tangible and intangible value delivered.

*Define:* **Strategic alignment (benefits management plan item)**

A measure of how well the project benefits align with existing business strategies.

---

*Define:* **Timeframe for realizing benefits (benefits management plan item)**

A rough estimate by phase, short-term, long-term or on-going.

---

*Define:* **Benefits owner (benefits management plan item)**

The person accountable for measuring and reporting value delivered.

---

*Define:* **Metrics (benefits management plan item)**

Results from the benefits owner measuring value.

---

*Define:* **Assumptions (benefits management plan item)**

A list of factors that must be true before we can succeed.

---

*Define:* **Risks (benefits management plan item)**

A list of things that might prevent us from succeeding.

---

# Chapter 5: The Environment

*Question:* **What are the 3 things that can influence a project?**

- Enterprise environment factors, or EEFs
- Organizational process assets, or OPAs
- Organizational systems

*Define:* **Enterprise environment factors, or EEFs**

Influences that come from outside of the project and often outside of the company itself.

*Define:* **Organizational process assets, or OPAs**

Influences that come from inside of a company, perhaps even other projects.

*Define:* **Organizational systems**

Influences based on the ability for people within a project to carry out needed actions.

*Question:* **What are some Internal EEFs?**

- Organizational culture, structure and governance
- Geographic distribution of facilities and resources
- Infrastructure
- Information technology software
- Resource availability
- Employee capability

*Question:* **What are some external EEFs?**

- Marketplace
- Social and cultural issues
- Laws
- Commercial databases
- Academic research
- Standards
- Finances
- The physical environment
- Exchange rates and inflation

*Question:* **What are the 2 groups of OPAs?**

- Processes, policies and procedures
- Knowledge repositories

*Define:* **Governance**

An arrangement at all levels of an organization that determine and influence employee's behavior.

*Question:* **What are the 4 domains that governance covers?**

- Alignment
- Risk
- Performance
- Communication

*Define:* **Management elements**

The various components that make up management in general within an organization, and are often assigned to specific people.

*Define:* **Organizational structure type**

Represents how an organization is arranged according to various views.

*Define:* **Project management office, or PMO**

The part of an organization that provides project governance and ensures sharing of resources, methodologies, tools and techniques.

*Question:* **What are the 3 types of PMOs?**

- Supportive
- Controlling
- Directive

*Define:* **Supportive PMO**

An entity that does not control a whole lot but does provide methodologies, tools and techniques for projects to use.

*Define:* **Controlling PMO**

An entity that asserts a moderate level of control by requiring compliance to things such as frameworks, methodologies, templates and governance frameworks.

*Define:* **Directive PMO**

An entity that exercises a high degree of control by assigning a project manager to directly manage each project, and to report back.

# Chapter 6: The Project Manager Role

---

*Question:* **What are the 3 spheres of influence a project manager has?**

- Project
- Organization
- Industry

---

*Question:* **What are the 2 most valuable skills a project manager can possess?**

The ability to build relationships and to communicate with a positive attitude.

---

*Question:* **What are the 3 project management competencies?**

- Technical project management
- Strategic or business management
- Leadership

---

*Define:* **Technical Project Management Skills**

The ability to apply project management knowledge to achieve the project goals.

---

*Define:* **Strategic or Business Management Skills**

The ability to see the high-level view of the organization and negotiate decisions within the project to meet that view.

---

*Define:* **Leadership Skills**

The ability to guide, motivate and direct the team to success.

---

*Define:* **Domain knowledge**

Knowledge specific to the organizational area or the industry needed to fully understand the why and how of the project.

---

*Define:* **Positional power**

Power derived from a formal position.

---

*Define:* **Informational power**

Power in which you control the flow of information.

---

*Define:* **Referent power**

Power gained when people respect you.

---

*Define:* **Situational power**

Power granted during a crisis.

---

*Define:* **Personal or charismatic power**

Power derived from charm or attraction.

---

*Define:* **Relational power**

Power gained from being associated with a network, connections or alliances.

---

*Define:* **Expert power**

Power in which you are a recognized expert.

---

*Define:* **Reward-oriented power**

Power in which you can give praise, or some other desired item.

---

*Define:* **Punitive power**

Power in which you can invoke discipline.

---

*Define:* **Ingratiating power**

Power executed by using flattery to win favor.

---

*Define:* **Pressure-based power**

Power in which you limit choice or movement to gain or receive compliance.

---

*Define:* **Guilt-based power**

Power in which you make people feel bad if they do not comply.

---

*Define:* **Persuasive power**

Power in which you convince someone to comply.

---

*Define:* **Avoiding power**

Power in which people comply out of the desire to avoid a negative experience with you.

---

*Define:* **Management**

The act of directing people to get from point A to point B using some set of rules.

---

*Define:* **Leadership**

The act of guiding people to the correct destination by using discussion and debate

---

*Question:* **What are the 6 different types of leadership style?**

- Laissez-faire
- Servant leader
- Transactional
- Transformational
- Charismatic
- Interactional

---

*Define:* **Laissez-faire leadership style**

A leadership style with a hands-off approach.

---

*Define:* **Servant leader leadership style**

A leadership style in which leadership is secondary and emerges after putting other people first.

---

*Define:* **Transactional leadership style**

A leadership style which rewards based on accomplishments.

---

*Define:* **Transformational leadership style**

A leadership style that transforms those who are led by inspiration and encouragement.

---

*Define:* **Charismatic leadership style**

A leadership style in which the leader inspires by using his or her personality.

---

*Define:* **Interactional leadership style**

A leadership style that is a combination of transactional, transformational and charismatic.

---

*Question:* **What are the 2 ways in which we can perform integration?**

- Integrating the organization's strategy with the project's goals
- Integrating processes, knowledge and people

---

*Define:* **Subject matter experts, or SMEs**

People who know all about their area, but might be ignorant when it comes to other areas

---

*Question:* **What are the 3 things that increase complexity?**

- System behavior
- Human behavior
- Ambiguity

---

*Define:* **System behavior**

Complexity that comes from the interactions between components and systems.

---

*Define:* **Human behavior**

Complexity that comes from interactions between diverse individuals or groups.

---

*Define:* **Ambiguity**

Complexity that comes from the lack of understanding of emerging issues.

---

*Question:* **What are the 4 attributes that can introduce complexity?**

- Multiple parts
- Multiple connections
- Dynamic interactions
- Interactions being far greater than the sum of the parts

---

*Define:* **Emergent behavior**

Occurs when the interactions between parts is far greater than the sum of the parts, resulting in increasing complexity.

24

# Section 2: Advanced Concepts

# Chapter 7: Analysis and Calculations

*Define:* **Earned value analysis (EVA)**

A technique that compares baselines to actual schedule and cost performance

*Define:* **Budget at completion (BAC)**

The amount of money estimated to have been spent by the time we complete the project.

*Define:* **Actual cost (AC)**

The actual budget spent by a given date.

*Define:* **Planned value (PV)**

The amount of money we expect the project to cost at a given time based on estimates.

*Question:* **What is the formula for earned value (EV)?**

EV = (% complete) x BAC

*Define:* **Variance analysis**

An analysis of how things change, most often dealing with cost and schedule changes.

*Question:* **What are the 4 types of variance analysis?**

- Schedule variance (SV)
- Cost variance (CV)
- Schedule performance index (SPI)
- Cost performance index (CPI)

*Question:* **What is the formula for schedule variance (SV) ?**

SV = EV – PV

*Question:* **How do you interpret the values of SV?**

- If SV < 0, we are behind schedule
- If SV = 0, we are right on-target
- If SV > 0, we are ahead of schedule

*Question:* **What is the formula for cost variance (CV) ?**

CV = EV – AC

*Question:* **How do you interpret the values of CV?**

- If CV < 0, we are behind schedule
- If CV = 0, we are right on-target
- If CV > 0, we are ahead of schedule

*Question:* **What is the formula for schedule performance index (SPI) ?**

SPI = EV / PV

---

*Question:* **How do you interpret the values of SPI?**

- If SPI < 1, we are behind schedule
- If SPI = 1, we are right on-target
- If SPI > 1, we are ahead of schedule

---

*Question:* **What is the formula for cost performance index (CPI) ?**

CPI = EV / AC

---

*Question:* **How do you interpret the values of CPI?**

- If CPI < 1, we are earning less than we spent
- If CPI = 1, earning and costs are the same – we're right on track
- If CPI > 1, we are earning more than we spent – this is good!

---

*Define:* **Trend analysis**

An analysis that tells us if the project performance is getting better or worse over time.

---

*Question:* **What are the 2 types of trend analysis?**

- Charts
- Forecasting

---

*Define:* **Chart trend analysis**

A graph that tracks PV, EV and AC.

---

*Define:* **Estimate at completion (EAC)**

A re-estimation of the total project cost when the BAC is deemed to be invalid.

---

*Define:* **Forecasting**

The process of calculating EAC.

---

*Define:* **Estimate to complete (ETC)**

An estimate of the amount of work left to be performed in the project.

---

*Question:* **What is the formula for estimating EAC?**

EAC = AC + Bottom-up ETC

---

*Question:* **What are the 3 methods for calculating EAC?**

- EAC = AC + BAC – EV
- EAC = BAC/CPI
- EAC = AC + [(BAC - EV) / (CPI x SPI)]

*Question:* **Which EAC calculation method assumes the best-case scenario?**

EAC = AC + BAC − EV

---

*Question:* **Which EAC calculation method is the most accurate?**

EAC = AC + [(BAC - EV) / (CPI x SPI)]

---

*Define:* **Variance at completion (VAC)**

VAC = BAC − EAC

---

*Define:* **Contingency reserve**

A reserve to account for known-unknowns in the schedule.

---

*Define:* **Schedule reserve**

Another name for the contingency reserve.

---

*Define:* **Management reserves**

A reserve to account for unknown-unknowns in the schedule.

---

*Define:* **Reserve analysis**

An analysis that looks at both contingency and management reserves and decides if they should grow or shrink.

---

*Define:* **To-complete performance index (TCPI)**

The future cost performance index (CPI) we must achieve for the remaining work, if you want to have any hope of staying within budget in terms of both time and money.

---

*Question:* **What is the TCPI formula to use if we are under-budget?**

TCPI = (BAC − EV) / (BAC − AC)

---

*Question:* **What is the TCPI formula to use if we are over-budget?**

TCPI = (BAC − EV) / (EAC − AC)

---

*Question:* **What is the difference between CPI and TCPI?**

CPI is the past cost performance of the project, while TCPI is the future cost performance of the project.

---

*Question:* **When would we use BAC when calculating TCPI?**

When we are under-budget.

---

*Question:* **When would we use EAC when calculating TCPI?**

When we are over-budget.

---

# Chapter 7: Analysis and Calculations

## 28

*Question:* **How do you interpret the values of TCPI?**

- If TCPI < 1, we are in great shape
- If TCPI > 1, we must perform with a better cost performance than the past cost performance OR get someone to approve a budget increase.
- If TCPI = 1, we can continue with the same cost performance.

# Chapter 8: Data Analysis

---

*Define:* **Data analysis**

Techniques in which we can sift through data collected during the project life cycle.

---

*Define:* **Alternatives analysis**

A data analysis technique that selects the corrective and preventative actions to implement when a deviation from a baseline happens.

---

*Define:* **Urgency risk parameter**

The amount of time we have for a response to be effective. A short period indicates high urgency.

---

*Define:* **Proximity risk parameter**

The amount of time we have before a risk might have an impact on one or more project goals. A short period indicates high proximity.

---

*Define:* **Dormancy risk parameter**

The amount of time we have after a risk has occurred before its impact is discovered. A short period indicates low dormancy.

---

*Define:* **Manageability risk parameter**

A measure of how easy it is for the risk owner to manage the occurrence or impact of a risk. Where management is high, manageability is high.

---

*Define:* **Controllability risk parameter**

A measure of how easy it is for the risk owner to control the risk's outcome. When the outcome is easily controlled, controllability is high.

---

*Define:* **Detectability risk parameter**

A measure of how easy it is to realize that a risk instance has occurred. When the risk occurrence can be easily detected, the dectability is high.

---

*Define:* **Connectivity risk parameter**

A measure of how closely a risk is related to other risks. When the risk is connected to many other risks, connectivity is high.

---

*Define:* **Strategic impact risk parameter**

The possibility the risk will have a negative or positive impact on the project goals. When the risk has a major impact, strategic impact is high.

---

*Define:* **Propinquity risk parameter**

A measure of how important the risk is to one or more stakeholders. When a risk is perceived to be very significant, propinquity is high.

---

*Define:* **Assumption and constraint analysis**

A data analysis technique that happens when we go over past assumptions and figure out the risk associated with each.

*Define:* **Cost-benefit analysis**

A data analysis technique that figures out the lowest cost way to correct deviations from a baseline.

*Define:* **Cost of quality analysis (COQ)**

A data analysis technique that makes some assumptions about the cost of quality that we can then use for estimating, including the cost of conforming or not conforming to certain quality standards.

*Question:* **What are the 3 costs addressed by COQ?**

- Prevention costs
- Appraisal costs
- Failure costs

*Define:* **Nonconformance**

Encountered when deliverables do not meet quality expectations.

*Define:* **Decision tree analysis**

A data analysis technique that is used to select the best option for multiple possible actions.

*Define:* **Document analysis**

A data analysis technique that reviews and assesses any relevant documents.

*Define:* **Earned value analysis (EVA)**

A data analysis technique that combines scope, schedule and cost to provide a comprehensive view of how the project is performing.

*Define:* **Influence diagram**

A data analysis technique that is a graphical tool used to decide action when the best option is uncertain.

*Define:* **Iteration burndown chart**

A data analysis technique that is a graphical chart tracking the amount of work not yet completed in the current iteration backlog.

*Define:* **Performance reviews**

A data analysis technique that analyzes how the schedule is going compared to the original baseline.

*Define:* **Process analysis**

A data analysis technique that identifies opportunities for process improvements.

*Define:* **Regression analysis**

A data analysis technique that analyzes the relationships between project variables on a past project to improve performance on future projects.

*Define:* **Reserve analysis**

A data analysis technique that figures out the proper amount of contingency and management reserves that are needed.

*Define:* **Risk data quality assessment analysis**

A data analysis technique that determines the accuracy of data we have on individual project risks, relative to a qualitative risk analysis.

*Define:* **Risk probability and impact assessment**

A data analysis technique that considers the likelihood that a specific risk will occur. Impacts will be negative for threats and positive for opportunities.

*Define:* **Root cause analysis (RCA)**

A data analysis technique that identifies the main cause of a problem.

*Define:* **Sensitivity analysis**

A data analysis technique that helps to determine which individual risks or other sources of uncertainty have the greatest potential impact on project goals.

*Define:* **Tornado diagram**

A sensitivity analysis for a risk showing how much impact it could have on project goals.

*Define:* **Simulation**

A data analysis technique that uses simulation models to figure out the impact on achieving our goals, based on individual project risks combined with other sources of uncertainty.

*Define:* **Monte Carlo analysis**

A type of simulation in which risks and uncertainty are used to calculate possible schedule outcomes.

*Define:* **Stakeholder analysis**

A data analysis technique that results in a list of stakeholders along with relevant information

*Question:* **What are the 5 areas included when documenting stake?**

- Interest
- Rights
- Ownership
- Knowledge
- Contribution

*Define:* **SWOT Analysis**

A data analysis technique that examines the project based on (s)trengths, (w)eaknesses, (o)pportunities and (t)hreats.

*Define:* **Technical performance analysis**

A data analysis technique that compares the date on which technical accomplishments were completed against the expected dates.

---

*Define:* **Trend analysis**

A data analysis technique that forecasts future performance based on past results, and is provided early enough so that teams can act before the impact is felt.

---

*Define:* **Variance analysis**

A data analysis technique that reviews the differences (or variance) between planned and actual performance.

---

*Define:* **What-if-scenario analysis**

A data analysis technique that is represented by asking 'What is the fallout if X happens?', and then seeing how it impacts the project schedule under different scenarios.

---

33

# Chapter 9: Data Gathering

*Define:* **Data Gathering**

The act of acquiring knowledge or ideas directly from people.

*Define:* **Benchmarking**

A data gathering technique which compares planned products and processes to similar companies who do the same.

*Define:* **Brainstorming**

A data gathering technique which gathers ideas and solutions from project team members.

*Define:* **Brain writing**

A refinement of brainstorming which allows participants to consider the questions before meeting.

*Define:* **Check list**

A data gathering technique in which a *list* is used to ensure we don't forget to *check* for something.

*Define:* **Check sheets**

A data gathering technique, also known as tally sheets, that is used to organize facts so that we can find potential quality problems, usually by tracking the frequency of repeating defect patterns.

*Define:* **Focus groups**

A data gathering technique which brings together a group of stakeholders to discuss project-related topics.

*Define:* **Interviews**

A data gathering technique in which we talk to an individual or group and ask specific questions.

*Define:* **Questionnaires and surveys**

A data gathering technique employing a written set of questions designed to quickly gather knowledge from many people.

*Define:* **Statistical sampling**

A data gathering technique in which a small subset is chosen for inspection and to verify quality.

# Chapter 10: Interpersonal and Team Skills

*Define:* **Interpersonal and team skills**

Soft skills that people within a project – usually the project manager – use to keep moving the process forward.

*Define:* **Active listening**

An interpersonal skill in which we acknowledge, clarify and confirm understanding.

*Define:* **Conflict management**

An interpersonal skill used to positively resolve conflicts.

*Question:* **What are the 5 methods of resolving conflicts?**

- Withdraw/avoid
- Smooth/accommodate
- Compromise/reconcile
- Force/redirect
- Collaborate/problem solve

*Define:* **Withdraw/avoid**

A conflict resolution method in which we retreat and postpone facing the issue.

*Define:* **Smooth/accommodate**

A conflict resolution method in which we emphasize areas of agreement over differences, and concede one's position to maintain harmony.

*Define:* **Compromise/reconcile**

A conflict resolution method in which we search for a solution that temporarily benefits everyone – usually a win/win scenario, but sometimes a lose-lose.

*Define:* **Force/redirect**

A conflict resolution method in which we force our viewpoint, resulting in a win-lose.

*Define:* **Collaborate/problem solve**

A conflict resolution method in which we have a cooperative attitude that leads to a long-term consensus and commitment – this is a real win-win.

*Define:* **Communication style assessment**

An interpersonal skill which looks at communication styles and identifies the preferred method. This is often used with unsupportive stakeholders.

*Define:* **Cultural awareness**

An interpersonal skill where we understand the differences between individuals and groups, and adapt our communication strategy to ensure understanding.

*Define:* **Decision making**

An interpersonal skill where we have the ability to negotiate and influence the organization and project team.

---

*Define:* **Emotional intelligence**

An interpersonal skill where we have the ability to understand and handle our own emotions, and that of other individuals and groups.

---

*Define:* **Influencing**

An interpersonal skill in which we have the ability to articulate, listen and persuade others without having the authority to force the desired decision.

---

*Define:* **Facilitation**

An interpersonal skill in which we use focus sessions to bring stakeholders together and produce requirements.

---

*Question:* **What are 3 examples of using facilitation interpersonal skills?**

- Joint application design/development (JAD)
- Quality function deployment (QDF)
- User stories

---

*Define:* **Joint application design/development (JAD)**

A type of facilitation skill used in the software development industry by bringing subject matter experts (SMEs) and the development team together.

---

*Define:* **Quality function deployment (QDF)**

A type of facilitation skill used in the manufacturing industry where customer needs are collected using the voice of the customer (VOC).

---

*Define:* **User stories**

A type of facilitation skill using short, textual descriptions of required functionality.

---

*Define:* **Leadership**

An interpersonal skill where we have the ability to lead a team and inspire them to do their jobs well.

---

*Define:* **Meeting management**

An interpersonal skill where we have the ability to set the agenda, ensure the proper attendees are present, and provide follow-up minutes and actions.

---

*Define:* **Motivation**

An interpersonal skill in which we provide a reason for someone to act.

---

*Define:* **Negotiation**

An interpersonal skill where we accommodate conflicting needs.

---

## 36

*Define:* **Networking**

An interpersonal skill where we interact with others to exchange information and develop contacts.

---

*Define:* **Political awareness**

An interpersonal skill where we become aware of both formal and informal power relationships, and discover how to communicate within those constraints.

---

*Define:* **Nominal group technique**

An interpersonal skill in which a voting process is used to rank the most useful brainstorming ideas.

---

*Question:* **What are the 5 steps used in the nominal group technique?**

- Ask a question and everyone writes down their answer
- A moderator writes down the ideas on a flip chart
- Each idea is discussed until everyone understands it
- Individuals rank the ideas, and the highest ranked are selected
- Repeat the entire process until we feel good about the outcome

---

*Define:* **Observation/conversation**

An interpersonal skill, also known as *job shadowing*, where an observer watches subjects as they go about their duties.

---

*Define:* **Team building**

An interpersonal skill in which we conduct activities to strengthen the team's social relations.

---

# Chapter 11: Project Documents

*Define:* **Project Documents**

An item used for both inputs and outputs for various processes, and represent whatever documents a process requires or produces.

*Define:* **Activity attributes**

A project document containing multiple attributes associated with each activity.

*Define:* **Activity list**

A project document that tracks all activities for the project.

*Define:* **Assumption log**

A project document that records all assumptions made during the project.

*Define:* **Basis of estimates**

A project document that indicates how estimates were derived and how each can be used.

*Define:* **Change log**

A project document that contains the status of all change requests.

*Define:* **Cost estimate**

A project document that calculates the money amount required to complete the project.

*Define:* **Cost forecasts**

A project document that is used to decide if the project is within a tolerable budget range based on past performance.

*Define:* **Duration estimates**

A project document that contains the number of required work periods to complete an activity.

*Define:* **Issue log**

A project document that records issues, who is responsible for resolving each, and by what date.

*Define:* **Lessons learned register**

A project document that records the things we have learned along the way, and keeps us from repeating mistakes.

*Define:* **Milestone list**

A project document that shows the dates for scheduled milestones.

*Define:* **Physical resource assignments**

A project document that records the material, equipment, supplies and locations for physical resources needed for the project.

*Define:* **Project calendars**

A project document that identifies working days and shifts that are available for scheduled activities.

*Define:* **Project communications**

A project document containing performance reports, the status of deliverables and other information generated by the project.

*Define:* **Project schedule**

A project document that shows linked activities with planned dates, durations, milestones and resources.

*Define:* **Project schedule network diagram**

A project document that contains the logical relationships between activities.

*Define:* **Project scope statement**

A project document that describes the work that will be performed and the work that is excluded, or out of scope.

*Define:* **Project team assignments**

A project document that assign people and resources to the team, after which the type of skills and experience are recorded.

*Define:* **Quality control measurements**

A project document that records the results of Control Quality activities and shows compliance.

*Define:* **Quality metrics**

A project document that links a project or product attribute to the Quality Control process.

*Define:* **Quality reports**

A project document that records quality management issues and recommendations.

*Define:* **Requirements documentation**

A project document that records all requirements that the project must meet.

*Define:* **Requirements traceability matrix**

A project document that links requirements to the associated deliverable.

*Define:* **Resource breakdown structure (RBS)**

A project document that includes information on the team makeup, and what knowledge may be available or missing.

*Define:* **Resource calendars**

A project document that specifies when and for how long resources will be available.

*Define:* **Resource requirements**

A project document listing all physical resources and people needed for a given activity.

*Define:* **Risk register**

A project document listing threats and opportunities that might impact the project.

*Define:* **Risk report**

A project document containing information on individual and overall project risk.

*Define:* **Schedule data**

A project document containing all data required to describe and control the schedule.

*Define:* **Schedule forecasts**

A project document used to decide if the project is within a tolerable schedule range, based on past performance.

*Define:* **Stakeholder register**

A project document that records information about stakeholders.

*Define:* **Team charter**

A project document that records how teams will operate together.

*Define:* **Test and evaluation documents**

A project document that is used to decide if we have achieved quality.

40

# Chapter 12: Project Management Plan

*Define:* **Project Management Plan**

A document describing how the project will be executed, monitored, controlled and closed.

*Question:* **What are the 3 portions of the project management plan?**

- Subsidiary management plans
- Baselines
- Additional components

*Define:* **Communications management plan**

A subsidiary project management plan describing how, when and by whom information will be conveyed.

*Define:* **Cost management plan**

A subsidiary project management plan describing how costs will be planned and controlled.

*Define:* **Procurement management plan**

A subsidiary project management plan describing how a project team will acquire goods and services from outside of the project.

*Define:* **Quality management plan**

A subsidiary project management plan describing how applicable policies will be implemented to achieve quality.

*Define:* **Requirements management plan**

A subsidiary project management plan describing how requirements will be analyzed, documented and managed.

*Define:* **Resource management plan**

A subsidiary project management plan describing how resources are acquired, allocated and controlled.

*Define:* **Risk management plan**

A subsidiary project management plan describing how risk management activities will be structured and performed.

*Define:* **Scope management plan**

A subsidiary project management plan describing how the scope will be defined and validated.

*Define:* **Stakeholder engagement plan**

A subsidiary project management plan identifying how we will keep stakeholders engaged throughout the project.

*Define:* **Schedule management plan**

A subsidiary project management plan that establishes the criteria and activities for developing and controlling the schedule.

*Question:* **What are the 9 components of the schedule management plan?**

- Project schedule model development
- Release and iteration length
- Level of accuracy
- Units of measure
- Organizational procedures links
- Project schedule model maintenance
- Control thresholds
- Rules of performance measurement
- Reporting formats

*Question:* **What are the 3 baselines in the project management plan?**

- Schedule baseline
- Scope baseline
- Cost baseline

*Define:* **Schedule baseline**

A project management plan baseline used to asses impacts to schedule changes.

*Define:* **Scope baseline**

A project management plan baseline providing the project and product definition.

*Define:* **Cost baseline**

A project management plan baseline used to asses impacts to project cost.

*Question:* **What are the 5 items in the project management plan additional components?**

- Change management plan
- Configuration management plan
- Development approach
- Performance measurement baseline
- Project life cycle description

*Define:* **Change management plan**

A project management plan additional component establishing the change control board (CCB), documents its authority, and describes how change control will be implemented.

*Define:* **Configuration management plan**

A project management plan additional component describing the configurable items of the project and which items will be updated.

*Define:* **Development approach**

A project management plan additional component used to create and evolve the project deliverable, such as predictive, iterative, incremental, agile or hybrid.

*Define:* **Performance measurement baseline**

A project management plan additional component used with the earned value analysis (EVA) and is compared with actual results to determine if action is needed.

*Define:* **Project life cycle description**

A project management plan additional component describing all phases the project passes through from start to completion.

# Chapter 13: Data Representation

*Define:* **Data Representation**

The various formats we can use to communicate information.

*Define:* **Affinity diagram**

A diagram allowing many ideas to be classified into groups.

*Define:* **Assignment matrix**

Also known as a responsibility assignment matrix (RAM), a technique that shows the project resources assigned to each work package, and can be created at multiple levels of detail.

*Define:* **RACI matrix**

A tool that defines duties such as (r)esponsible, (a)ccountable, (c)onsulted and (i)nformed.

*Define:* **Cause-and-effect diagram**

Also known as a fishbone diagram, a why-why diagram, or an Ishikawa diagram, a tool that breaks down the causes of a problem into branches and points to the single root cause.

*Define:* **Control chart**

A tool to figure out if a process is stable or has a predictable performance using specification and control limits.

*Define:* **Specification limits**

A tool used with a control chart to define acceptable values.

*Define:* **Control limits**

Statistically calculated values used with a control chart to define lower and upper expectations, and when exceeded action should be taken to restore quality.

*Define:* **Directions of influence**

A tool that classifies stakeholders based on their influence on the project.

*Question:* **What are the 4 directions of influence?**

- Upward
- Downward
- Outward
- Sideward

*Define:* **Flowchart**

Also called a process map, a tool that displays the sequence of steps and branches that result when we transform an output of one process into an input of one or more other processes

## 44

*Define:* **Horizontal value chain**

The result of process outputs providing input into one or more other processes.

*Define:* **SIPOC**

A version of a value chain representing (s)uppliers, (i)nputs, (p)rocesses, (o)utputs and (c)ustomers.

*Define:* **Hierarchical chart**

A tool used to show organizational positions and relationships.

*Question:* **What are the 3 different manners in which a hierarchical chart is used?**

- Work breakdown structures (WBS)
- Organizational breakdown structures (OBS)
- Resource breakdown structures (RBS)

*Define:* **Work breakdown structures (WBS)**

A tool that illustrates how project deliverables are broken down into work packages, and shows areas of responsibility.

*Define:* **Organizational breakdown structures (OBS)**

A tool that illustrates how the organization's departments are broken down, with activities or work packages listed for each department.

*Define:* **Resource breakdown structures (RBS)**

A hierarchical lists of teams and physical resources grouped by category and resource type.

*Define:* **Histogram**

A graphical representation of numerical data.

*Define:* **Logical data mapping**

A visual representation of data, and is described in a business language that is technology-agnostic.

*Define:* **Matrix diagram**

A table consisting of columns and rows, and allows us to identify the strength of relationships between different factors and goals.

*Define:* **Mind mapping**

A tool that consolidates ideas generated using brainstorming into a single map to illustrate commonality and differences.

*Define:* **Prioritization of stakeholders**

The process of ranking stakeholder importance for projects with many stakeholders.

*Define:* **Probability and impact matrix**

A grid mapping the probability of each risk occurrence and the resulting impact on project goals.

*Define:* **Salience model**

Describes stakeholders based on their power or authority, urgency and legitimacy.

*Define:* **Scatter diagram**

A graph showing the relationship between two variables, with quality defects on one axis.

*Define:* **Stakeholder cube**

A 3-dimensional model depicting stakeholders which helps with decisions on communication strategies.

*Define:* **Stakeholder engagement assignment matrix**

A tool that compares the current level of stakeholder engagement to the level needed for a successful project.

*Question:* **What are the 5 engagement levels of the stakeholder engagement assignment matrix?**

- Unaware
- Resistant
- Neutral
- Supportive
- Leading

*Define:* **Unaware engagement level**

The stakeholder is not aware of the project or potential impacts.

*Define:* **Resistant engagement level**

A stakeholder engagement level in which the stakeholder is aware of the project but does not want the changes that will result.

*Define:* **Neutral engagement level**

A stakeholder engagement level in which the stakeholder is aware of the project but simply doesn't care.

*Define:* **Supportive engagement level**

A stakeholder engagement level in which the stakeholder is aware of the project and is supportive of the outcomes.

*Define:* **Leading engagement level**

A stakeholder engagement level in which the stakeholder is aware of the project and is actively engaged in ensuring the project is successful.

*Define:* **Text-oriented format**

Also known as a position description or role-responsibility-authority form, an information format that details team member responsibilities in text-form.

*Define:* **Power/interest grid, power/influence grid, or impact/influence grid**

A tool that groups stakeholders according to 4 levels, which are power, interest, influence and impact.

46

*Define:* **Power grid level**

The authority a stakeholder possesses.

---

*Define:* **Interest grid level**

The level of concern a stakeholder has about the project outcome.

---

*Define:* **Influence grid level**

The ability a stakeholder has to affect the project outcome.

---

*Define:* **Impact grid level**

The ability a stakeholder has to cause project changes.

---

47

# Section 3: Knowledge Areas

*Question:* **What are the three sections within each process?**

- Inputs
- Tools and Techniques
- Outputs

*Define:* **Input process section**

The artifacts that are required or optional for the process to start.

*Define:* **Tools and Techniques process section**

Skills used to execute the process.

*Define:* **Output process section**

A list of items the process creates.

# Chapter 14: Project Integration Management

*Question:* **What are the 7 processes (in order) for the project integration management knowledge area?**

- Develop the project charter
- Develop the project management plan
- Direct and manage the project work
- Manage the project knowledge
- Monitor and control the project work
- Perform integrated change control
- Close the project or phase

*Define:* **Develop project charter process**

The process where we create a document that authorizes the project and project manager.

*Define:* **Develop project management plan process**

The process where we take all the various plan components and put them into a single plan.

*Define:* **Direct and manage project work process**

The process where we do the actual work.

*Define:* **Manage project knowledge process**

The process where we gather and track existing knowledge and new knowledge generated by the project.

*Define:* **Monitor and control project work process**

The process where we monitor and report how things are going.

*Define:* **Perform integrated change control process**

The process where we approve or deny any late-breaking change requests.

*Question:* **What are some tailoring opportunities for the project integration management knowledge area?**

- Project life cycle
- Development life cycle
- Management approaches
- Knowledge management
- Change
- Lessons learned
- Benefits

*Define:* **Accepted Deliverables**

Project outputs that include approved product specs, delivery receipts or work performance documents – whatever is produced by the project, and is validated by the stakeholder as meeting their requirements.

*Define:* **Agreements**

A documentation of the initial intentions for the project, in the form of contracts, memorandums of understanding (MOUs), service level agreements (SLAs), verbal agreements or email.

*Define:* **Approved Change Requests**

Change requests made after the project has been initiated that have been approved by the project manager or the change control board (CCB).

---

*Define:* **Assumption Log**

A repository that contains all high-level and detailed assumptions made during the project, as well as any constraints that are encountered.

---

*Define:* **Business Documents**

A document that reference 2 other documents – the business case and the benefits management plan.

---

*Define:* **Change Control Tools**

Tools used to approve or reject change requests.

---

*Question:* **What are the 7 activities involved with the change control tools ITTO?**

- Identify configuration item
- Record and report configuration item status
- Perform configuration item verification and audit
- Identify changes
- Document changes
- Decide on changes
- Track changes

---

*Define:* **Change Requests**

A formal proposal to modify a document, deliverable or baseline.

---

*Define:* **What are the 4 types of change requests?**

- Corrective action
- Preventative action
- Defect repair
- Updates

---

*Define:* **Corrective action change request**

An action that realigns work with the project plan after something has happened.

---

*Define:* **Preventative action change request**

An action that realigns work with the project plan before something bad happens.

---

*Define:* **Defect repair change request**

An action resulting in a modification of a product or component that does not conform.

---

*Define:* **Updates change request**

An action that makes changes to control documents.

---

## 50

*Define:* **Data Analysis**

Various ways in which we can sift through data collected during the project life cycle.

*Define:* **Data Gathering**

The act of acquiring knowledge or ideas directly from people.

*Define:* **Decision Making**

Techniques by which we select actions to take.

*Question:* **What are the 3 decision making techniques?**

- Autocratic decision making
- Multicriteria decision analysis
- Voting

*Define:* **Autocratic decision making**

A decision-making technique in which one individual decides for the group.

*Define:* **Multicriteria decision analysis**

A decision-making technique using a decision matrix to help arrive at a decision.

*Define:* **Voting**

A decision-making technique comprised of 3 types – unanimity, majority and plurality.

*Define:* **Unanimity voting**

A decision-making technique in which a decision is reached by everyone.

*Define:* **Majority voting**

A decision-making technique in which a decision is reached by more than 50% of voters.

*Define:* **Plurality voting**

A decision-making technique in which a decision is reached by the largest block of voters, even if they don't represent more than 50% of all voters.

*Define:* **Data Representation**

The various formats we can use to communicate information.

*Define:* **Deliverables**

A product or result that must be created before a process can be called complete.

*Define:* **Expert Judgement**

The ability to use good judgement based on expertise.

51

*Define:* **Final Product, Service or Result Transition**

An action that moves the project output from one team to another.

*Define:* **Final Report**

A report that provides a summary of the project performance.

*Define:* **Information Management**

The act of creating information and connecting people to this new information.

*Define:* **Interpersonal and Team Skills**

Soft skills that people within a project – usually the project manager – use to keep moving the process forward.

*Define:* **Issue Log**

A document that tracks all problems, gaps, inconsistencies or conflicts that must be addressed so a negative impact does not result.

*Define:* **Knowledge Management**

The act of using certain tools and techniques to connect people such that they create new knowledge, share existing knowledge and integrate the knowledge of all team members together.

*Question:* **What are examples of knowledge management?**

- Networking
- Meetings
- Shadowing
- Focus groups
- Training

*Define:* **Lessons Learned Register**

A knowledge repository for information learned during the project that describes a situation, and includes the impact, recommendations and proposed actions.

*Define:* **Organizational Process Assets Updates**

Occurs when organizational process assets are updated.

*Question:* **What are 4 types of OPA Updates?**

- Organizational standard policies, processes and procedures
- Personnel administration
- Organizational communication requirements
- Formal knowledge-sharing and information-sharing procedures

*Define:* **Outputs from Other Processes**

A generic way of saying other processes will provide various inputs.

*Define:* **Procurement Documentation**

Documentation that is required before a project can be closed out.

*Define:* **Project Charter**

The document that both authorizes a project and gives the project manager the authority to obtain the required resources.

*Define:* **Project Documents**

Represent whatever documents a process requires or produces.

---

*Define:* **Project Documents Updates**

Occur when any project document is updated.

---

*Define:* **Project Management Information System (PMIS)**

Provides access to software tools, and can include gathering and reporting Key Performance Indicators (KPIs).

---

*Question:* **What tools does a PMIS use to distribute information?**

- Electronic project management tools
- Electronic communications management
- Social media management

---

*Define:* **Project Management Plan**

A document describing how the project will be executed, monitored, controlled and closed.

---

*Define:* **Project Management Plan Updates**

Any change to the project management plan that goes through the change control process.

---

*Define:* **Work Performance Data**

The raw observations and measurements collected while work is underway.

---

*Define:* **Work Performance Information**

The result of comparing work performance data to documents or project components, and is used to determine how well the project is proceeding.

---

*Define:* **Work Performance Reports**

Results when work performance information is put into a physical or electronic form.

---

*Question:* **What 2 things does the develop project charter officially accomplish?**

- Authorize the existence of a project.
- Give the project manager authority to use the required resources.

---

*Question:* **Is the charter a contract?**

No because no money or resources change hands.

---

*Question:* **What process category does the develop charter process belong to?**

Once or at predefined points.

## 54

*Question:* **What are the inputs to the develop charter process?**

- Business Documents
- Agreements
- EEFs
- OPAs

---

*Question:* **What are the tools and techniques for the develop charter process?**

- Expert Judgement
- Data Gathering
- Interpersonal and team skills
- Meetings

---

*Question:* **What are the outputs of the develop charter process?**

- Project Charter
- Assumption Log

---

*Question:* **What process category does the Develop Project Management Plan process belong to?**

Once or at predefined points.

---

*Question:* **What are the inputs to the Develop Project Management Plan process?**

- Project Charter
- Outputs from Other Processes
- EEFs
- OPAs

---

*Question:* **What are the tools and techniques for the Develop Project Management Plan process?**

- Expert Judgement
- Data Gathering
- Interpersonal and team skills
- Meetings

---

*Question:* **What are the outputs of the Develop Project Management Plan process?**

- Project Management Plan

---

*Question:* **What process category does the Direct and Manage Project Work process belong to?**

Throughout the project.

---

*Question:* **What are the inputs to the Direct and Manage Project Work process?**

- Project Management
- Project Documents
- Approved Change Requests
- EEFs
- OPAs

---

*Question:* **What are the tools and techniques for the Direct and Manage Project Work process?**

- Project Management Information System (PMIS)
- Meetings

---

*Question:* **What are the outputs of the Direct and Manage Project Work process?**

- Deliverables
- Work Performance Data
- Issue Log
- Change Requests
- Project Management Plan Updates
- Project Documents Updates
- Organizational Process Assets Updates

---

*Question:* **What process category does the Manage Project Knowledge process belong to?**

Throughout the project.

---

*Question:* **What are the inputs to the Manage Project Knowledge process?**

- Project Management Plan
- Project Documents
- Deliverables
- EEFs
- OPAs

---

*Question:* **What are the tools and techniques for the Manage Project Knowledge process?**

- Expert Judgement
- Knowledge Management
- Information Management
- Interpersonal and Team Skills

---

*Question:* **What are the outputs of the Manage Project Knowledge process?**

- Lessons Learned Register
- Project Management Plan Updates
- Organizational Process Assets Updates

---

*Question:* **What process category does the Monitor and Control Project Work process belong to?**

Throughout the project.

---

*Question:* **What are the inputs to the Monitor and Control Project Work process?**

- Project Management Plan
- Project Documents
- Work Performance Information
- Agreements
- EEFs
- OPAs

---

*Question:* **What are the tools and techniques for the Monitor and Control Project Work process?**

- Expert Judgement
- Data Analysis
- Decision Making
- Meetings

---

*Question:* **What are the outputs of the Monitor and Control Project Work process?**

- Work Performance Reports
- Change Requests
- Project Management Plan Updates
- Project Documents Updates

*Question:* **What process category does the Perform Integrated Change Control process belong to?**

Throughout the project.

*Question:* **What are the inputs to the Perform Integrated Change Control process?**

- Project Management Plan
- Project Documents
- Work Performance Reports
- Change Requests
- EEFs
- OPAs

*Question:* **What are the tools and techniques for the Perform Integrated Change Control process?**

- Expert Judgement
- Change Control Tools
- Data Analysis
- Decision Making
- Meetings

*Question:* **What are the outputs of the Perform Integrated Change Control process?**

- Approved Change Requests
- Project Management Plan Updates
- Project Documents Updates

*Question:* **What process category does the Close Project or Phase process belong to?**

Once or at predefined points.

*Question:* **What are the inputs to the Close Project or Phase process?**

- Project Charter
- Project Management Plan
- Project Documents
- Accepted Deliverables
- Business Documents
- Agreements
- Procurement Documentation
- OPAs

*Question:* **What are the tools and techniques for the Close Project or Phase process?**

- Expert Judgement
- Data Analysis
- Meetings

*Question:* **What are the outputs of the Close Project or Phase process?**

- Project Documents Updates
- Final Product, Service, or Result Transition
- Final Report
- OPAs

# Chapter 15: Project Scope Management

*Question:* **What are the 6 processes for the Project Scope Management knowledge area?**

- Plan Scope Management
- Collect Requirements
- Define Scope
- Create WBS
- Validate Scope
- Control Scope

*Define:* **Plan Scope Management Process**

The process where we create the plan to document scope.

*Define:* **Collect Requirements Process**

The process where we collect and document requirements.

*Define:* **Define Scope Process**

The process where we create a detailed description of the project.

*Define:* **Create WBS Process**

The process where we divide deliverables into smaller components.

*Define:* **Validate Scope Process**

The process where we formalize acceptance of the deliverables.

*Define:* **Control Scope Process**

The process where we monitor scope and manage changes to the scope baseline.

*Question:* **What are the 2 types of scope?**

- Product scope
- Project scope

*Define:* **Product scope**

The features and functions of a product.

*Define:* **Project scope**

The work performed to deliver the product in-scope.

*Question:* **What are the 5 ways we can customize the Project Scope Management knowledge area?**

- Knowledge and requirements management
- Validation and control
- Development approach
- Stability of requirements
- Governance

*Define:* **Context Diagram**

An example of a scope model, and visually illustrates how the business system - processes, equipment, computer systems, etc. – interact with people and other systems.

*Define:* **Data Representation**

Various formats we can use to communicate information.

*Define:* **Decomposition**

Occurs when we break down project scope into more manageable components.

*Define:* **Work package**

A WBS component where cost and duration can be estimated.

*Define:* **Epic**

Higher-level components when using an agile methodology.

*Define:* **Rolling wave planning**

An estimation and requirements approach where we wait until the WBS is developed to decompose components.

*Define:* **100% rule**

The act of rolling up all product and project work into higher levels so that nothing is left out.

*Define:* **Inspection**

Activities such as measuring, examining and validating to ensure deliverables meet the acceptance criteria.

*Define:* **Product Analysis**

Defining products and services, by asking questions and forming answers to help describe what is going to be delivered.

*Define:* **Project Scope Statement**

A document that includes the description of the project scope, major deliverables, assumptions and constraints.

*Question:* **What 4 topics are included in the project scope statement?**

- Product scope description
- Deliverables
- Acceptance criteria
- Project exclusions

*Define:* **Project Scope Document**

A document containing a detailed description of the project scope, major deliverables, assumptions and constraints.

*Define:* **Prototypes**

A mock-up or simulation of the final product.

*Define:* **Storyboarding**

A prototyping technique using images or illustrations.

*Define:* **Requirements Documentation**

A document describing how individual requirements meet some need for the project.

*Question:* **What are the 6 types of requirements documentation?**

- Business requirements
- Stakeholder requirements
- Solution requirements
- Transition and readiness requirements
- Project requirements
- Quality requirements

*Define:* **Business requirements**

A requirements document that describes the highest-level needs and explains why a project exists.

*Define:* **Stakeholder requirements**

A requirements document describing the needs of the stakeholders.

*Define:* **Solution requirements**

A requirements document describing the project deliverables.

*Question:* **What are the 2 groups of solution requirements?**

- Functional requirements
- Nonfunctional requirements

*Define:* **Functional requirements**

A requirements document describing the behaviors of the product.

*Define:* **Nonfunctional requirements**

A requirements document describing the environmental conditions required for the product to be useful.

*Define:* **Transition and readiness requirements**

A requirements document describing temporary capabilities needed to go from as-is to the desired future state.

*Define:* **Project requirements**

A requirements document describing the actions and processes the project needs to meet.

*Define:* **Quality requirements**

A requirements document capturing any condition or criteria that must be met for the project to be declared a success.

*Define:* **Requirements Management Plan**

A document defining how product requirements will be collected, documented and maintained, and is sometimes called a business analysis plan.

*Question:* **What are the 5 components of the requirements management plan?**

- How requirement activities are carried out
- Configuration change activities
- How requirements will be prioritized
- Which metrics will be used
- How requirements will be tracked on the traceability matrix

*Define:* **Requirements Traceability Matrix**

A grid that maps requirements to one or more deliverables.

*Define:* **Scope Baseline**

The approved version of the scope statement, WBS, and the WBS dictionary.

*Question:* **What are the 6 components of the scope baseline?**

- Project scope statement
- WBS
- Control account
- Planning package
- Work package
- WBS Dictionary

*Define:* **Project scope statement**

The description of the project scope, major deliverables, assumptions and constraints.

*Define:* **WBS**

A hierarchical decomposition of the work to be done.

*Define:* **Control account**

A WBS control point where scope, budget and schedule are measured. A control account can have one or more planning packages.

*Define:* **Planning package**

A WBS component that belongs to a control account and has one or more work packages. It has known work content, but is not scheduled.

*Define:* **Work package**

The lowest level of the WBS with a unique identifier, and can be scheduled.

---

*Define:* **WBS Dictionary**

A document that provides details for every component in the WBS.

---

*Define:* **Scope management plan**

A document describing how scope will be defined, monitored and validated.

---

*Question:* **What are the 4 components of the scope management plan?**

- Preparing a scope statement
- Creating the WBS from the scope statement
- Deciding how the scope baseline will be approved and maintained
- Deciding how the acceptance of deliverables will happen

---

*Define:* **Verified Deliverables**

Project deliverables that are complete and have been checked for correctness using the Control Quality process.

---

*Question:* **What process category does the Plan Scope Management process belong to?**

Once or at predefined points.

---

*Question:* **What are the inputs to the Plan Scope Management process?**

- Project Charter
- Project Management Plan
- EEFs
- OPAs

---

*Question:* **What are the tools and techniques for the Plan Scope Management process?**

- Expert Judgement
- Data Analysis
- Meetings

---

*Question:* **What are the outputs of the Plan Scope Management process?**

- Scope Management Plan
- Requirements Management Plan

---

*Question:* **What process category does the Collect Requirements process belong to?**

Once or at predefined points.

---

*Question:* **What are the inputs to the Collect Requirements process?**

- Project Charter
- Project Management Plan
- Project Documents
- Business Documents
- Agreements
- EEFs
- OPAs

*Question:* **What are the tools and techniques for the Collect Requirements process?**

- Expert Judgement
- Data Gathering
- Data Analysis
- Decision Making
- Data Representation
- Interpersonal and Team Skills
- Context Diagram
- Prototypes

*Question:* **What are the outputs of the Collect Requirements process?**

- Requirements Documentation
- Requirements Traceability Matrix

*Question:* **What process category does the Define Scope process belong to?**

Once or at predefined points.

*Question:* **What are the inputs to the Define Scope process?**

- Project Charter
- Project Management Plan
- Project Documents
- EEFs
- OPAs

*Question:* **What are the tools and techniques for the Define Scope process?**

- Expert Judgement
- Data Analysis
- Decision Making
- Interpersonal and Team Skills
- Product Analysis

*Question:* **What are the outputs of the Define Scope process?**

- Project Scope Statement
- Project Documents Updates

*Question:* **What process category does the Create WBS process belong to?**

Once or at predefined points.

*Question:* **What are the inputs to the Create WBS process?**

- Project Management Plan
- Project Documents
- EEFs
- OPAs

*Question:* **What are the tools and techniques for the Create WBS process?**

- Expert Judgement
- Decomposition

*Question:* **What are the outputs of the Create WBS process?**

- Scope Baseline
- Project Documents Updates

*Question:* **What process category does the Validate Scope process belong to?**

Throughout the project.

*Question:* **What are the inputs to the Validate Scope process?**

- Project Management Plan
- Project Documents
- Verified Deliverables
- Work Performance Data

*Question:* **What are the tools and techniques for the Validate Scope process?**

- Inspection
- Decision Making

*Question:* **What are the outputs of the Validate Scope process?**

- Accepted Deliverables
- Work Performance Information
- Change Requests
- Project Documents Updates

*Define:* **Scope creep**

The uncontrolled expansion to project or product scope.

*Question:* **What process category does the Control Scope process belong to?**

Throughout the project.

*Question:* **What are the inputs to the Control Scope process?**

- Project Management Plan
- Project Documents
- Work Performance Data
- OPAs

65

*Question:* **What are the tools and techniques for the Control Scope process?**

- Data Analysis

*Question:* **What are the outputs of the Control Scope process?**

- Work Performance Information
- Change Requests
- Project Management Plan Updates
- Project Documents Updates

# Chapter 16: Project Schedule Management

*Question:* **What are the 6 processes for Project Schedule Management?**

- Plan Schedule Management
- Define Activities
- Sequence Activities
- Estimate Activity Durations
- Develop Schedule
- Control Schedule

*Define:* **Plan Schedule Management Process**

The project schedule management process establishing how we will manage the project schedule.

*Define:* **Define Activities Process**

The project schedule management process where we identify and document the activities required to create the project deliverables.

*Define:* **Sequence Activities Process**

The project schedule management process where we figure out relationships between the activities.

*Define:* **Estimate Activity Durations Process**

The project schedule management process where we figure out how many work periods it will take for all activities to be completed.

*Define:* **Develop Schedule Process**

The project schedule management process which produces a calendar schedule based on resources, activity relationships and activity dates.

*Define:* **Control Schedule Process**

The project schedule management process where we watch the schedule and handle any changes.

*Define:* **Adaptive planning**

Occurs when we acknowledge that priorities may change after work starts and flex accordingly.

*Question:* **What are the 2 flavors of adaptive planning?**

- Iterative scheduling with a backlog
- On-demand scheduling

*Define:* **Iterative scheduling with a backlog**

A type of rolling wave planning such as an agile approach.

*Define:* **On-demand scheduling**

A technique most commonly represented as Kanban in which we want to minimize the amount of work in-progress at any given time.

*Question:* **What are the 4 areas we can tailor for the project schedule management knowledge area?**

- Life cycle approach
- Resource availability
- Project dimensions
- Technology support

---

*Define:* **Activity Attributes**

Information attached to activities, extending the amount of information we can associate with each activity.

---

*Define:* **Activity List**

A list of all scheduled activities in the entire project.

---

*Define:* **Agile Release Planning**

A high-level project timeline based on the roadmap, providing an estimate of the number of iterations that will be required for the release.

---

*Define:* **Analogous Estimating**

A method for estimating activity duration or cost using historical data from a similar activity or project.

---

*Define:* **Basis of Estimates**

A document describing how an estimate was arrived at, including assumptions, constraints, range of possible values and confidence level.

---

*Define:* **Bottom-Up Estimating**

The act of decomposing activities into smaller components, which are then estimated, and then summing all of them up into a single estimate.

---

*Define:* **Critical Path Method**

The act of examining a project schedule and calculating the shortest possible time in which the project could be completed.

---

*Define:* **Float**

The amount to which a scheduled activity can be delayed from its start date without impacting the project finish date.

---

*Define:* **Zero total float**

A term describing any activity delay that would cause a delay in the overall project.

---

*Define:* **Positive total float**

A term describing any activity that can slip a little without impacting the project's overall completion date.

---

*Define:* **Negative float**

A term describing any activity that will not complete until after the project's desired completion date.

---

*Question:* **What are the 4 attributes used with dependency determination and integration?**

- Mandatory
- Discretionary
- External
- Internal

---

*Define:* **Mandatory dependency**

Occurs when a predecessor must be completed before the successor is possible.

---

*Define:* **Discretionary dependency**

Occurs when a best practice should be followed, but is not strictly enforced.

---

*Define:* **External dependency**

Occurs when there is a dependency on an activity external to the project.

---

*Define:* **Internal dependency**

Occurs when there is a dependency on an activity internal to the project.

---

**What are the combination of attributes allowed with dependency determination and integration?**

- Mandatory External
- Mandatory Internal
- Discretionary External
- Discretionary Internal

---

*Define:* **Duration Estimates**

A quantitative calculation resulting in the number of time periods required to complete an activity.

---

*Define:* **Lead**

The amount of time that a successor activity can get an early start relative to the finish date of the predecessor activity.

---

*Define:* **Lag**

The amount of time that must elapse after the predecessor starts before the successor can start.

---

*Define:* **Milestone List**

A list of significant points or events in a project.

---

*Define:* **Parametric Estimating**

An estimating technique that uses an algorithm using historical data and a multiplier to reflect project size.

---

*Define:* **Precedence Diagramming Method (PDM)**

A visual representation of how activities are linked together, including the sequence of execution.

*Question:* **What are the 4 types of relationships defined with PDM?**

- Finish-to-start (FS)
- Finish-to-finish (FF)
- Start-to-start (SS)
- Start-to-finish (SF)

*Define:* **Finish-to-start (FS) PDM relationship**

An activity relationship in which a successor cannot start until its predecessor finishes.

*Define:* **Finish-to-finish (FF) PDM relationship**

An activity relationship in which a successor cannot finish until its predecessor finishes.

*Define:* **Start-to-start (SS) PDM relationship**

An activity relationship in which a successor cannot start until its predecessor starts.

*Define:* **Start-to-finish (SF) PDM relationship**

An activity relationship in which a successor cannot finish until its predecessor starts.

*Define:* **Project Calendars**

Documents that identify working days and shifts that are available for scheduled activities.

*Define:* **Project Schedule**

An artifact showing linked activities with planned dates, durations, milestones and resources.

*Define:* **Target project schedule**

An artifact containing dates for activities before estimations occur.

*Question:* **What are the 3 methods used to show a project schedule?**

- Bar chart, also called a Gantt chart
- Milestone chart
- Project schedule network diagram

*Define:* **Bar chart**

A tool that displays activities on the Y axis and dates on the X axis.

*Define:* **Milestone chart**

A tool similar to a bar chart, but contains only major deliverables and key external interfaces, as opposed to all activities.

*Define:* **Project Schedule Network Diagrams**

A visual picture showing the various dependencies between activities, and serves to highlight risky activities.

# Chapter 16: Project Schedule Management

*Define:* **Resource Optimization**

The act of adjusting the start and finish dates of an activity to optimize the availability of the required resources

*Question:* **What 2 techniques are used with resource optimization?**

- Resource leveling
- Resource smoothing

*Define:* **Resource leveling**

The act of adjusting activity dates due to insufficient resources during the activity's execution time.

*Define:* **Resource smoothing**

The same as resource leveling but is carried out in such a way that does not impact critical paths or the project's completion date.

*Define:* **Rolling Wave Planning**

An iterative planning technique in which the near-term work is planned in detail, while work further in the future is only planned at a high-level.

*Define:* **Schedule Compression**

Techniques used to shorten the project timeline without impacting scope.

*Question:* **What 2 variations are used to compress the schedule?**

- Crashing
- Fast tracking

*Define:* **Crashing**

The act of adding additional resources by bringing in additional bodies, allowing overtime, or paying to expedite activities on the critical path.

*Define:* **Fast tracking**

The act of performing work in parallel that was originally scheduled to be sequential.

*Define:* **Schedule Data**

All data required to describe and control the schedule.

*Question:* **At a minimum, what items does schedule data include?**

- Milestones
- Activities
- Activity attributes
- Assumptions and constraints

*Define:* **Schedule Forecasts**

Updates to a schedule calculated based on work performance information, and are issued as changes are made, or specific events are reached.

# Chapter 16: Project Schedule Management

*Define:* **Schedule Network Analysis**

A activity that generates the project schedule by using the critical path method, resource optimization and modeling.

*Define:* **Three-Point Estimating**

An approach to estimation that takes the average of 3 data points – pessimistic (tP), most likely (tM), and optimistic (tO).

*Define:* **Triangular distribution**

A three-point estimating technique with each case being represented equally: $tE = (tP + tO + tM)/3$.

*Define:* **Beta distribution**

A three-point estimating technique that emphasizes the most likely case: $tE = (tP + tO + 4tM)/6$.

*Define:* **What process category does the Plan Schedule Management process belong to?**

Once or at predefined points.

*Question:* **What are the inputs to the Plan Schedule Management process?**

- Project Charter
- Project Management Plan
- EEFs
- OPAs

*Question:* **What are the tools and techniques for the Plan Schedule Management process?**

- Expert Judgement
- Data Analysis
- Meetings

*Question:* **What are the outputs of the Plan Schedule Management process?**

- Schedule Management Plan

*Question:* **What process category does the Define Activities process belong to?**

Throughout the project.

*Question:* **What are the inputs to the Define Activities process?**

- Project Management Plan
- EEFs
- OPAs

*Question:* **What are the tools and techniques for the Define Activities process?**

- Expert Judgement
- Decomposition
- Rolling Wave Planning
- Meetings

*Question:* **What are the outputs of the Define Activities process?**

- Activity List
- Activity Attributes
- Milestone List
- Change Requests
- Project Management Plan Updates

---

*Question:* **What process category does the Sequence Activities process belong to?**

Throughout the project.

---

*Question:* **What are the inputs to the Sequence Activities process?**

- Project Management Plan
- Project Documents
- EEFs
- OPAs

---

*Question:* **What are the tools and techniques for the Sequence Activities process?**

- Precedence Diagramming Method
- Dependency Determination and Integration
- Leads and Lags
- Project Management Information System (PMIS)

---

*Question:* **What are the outputs of the Sequence Activities process?**

- Project Schedule Network Diagrams
- Project Documents Updates

---

*Question:* **What 4 factors should we consider when estimating duration?**

- The law of diminishing returns
- Number of resources
- Advances in technology
- Motivation of staff

---

*Define:* **Law of diminishing returns**

A law that states while increasing one factor will decrease estimates, there is a point at which the more the factor is increased, the less positive impact it has.

---

*Define:* **Number of resources**

A principal recognizing that doubling the number of resources does not in fact reduce the time by half.

---

*Define:* **Student syndrome**

A principal recognizing that people only apply themselves at the last possible moment

---

*Define:* **Parkinson's Law**

A principal recognizing that work expands to fill the time available

---

*Define:* **What process category does the Estimate Activity Duration process belong to?**

Throughout the project.

*Question:* **What are the inputs to the Estimate Activity Duration process?**

- Project Management Plan
- Project Documents
- EEFs
- OPAs

*Question:* **What are the tools and techniques for the Estimate Activity Duration process?**

- Expert Judgement
- Analogous Estimating
- Parametric Estimating
- Three-Point Estimating
- Bottom-Up Estimating
- Data Analysis
- Decision Making
- Meetings

*Question:* **What are the outputs of the Estimate Activity Duration process?**

- Duration Estimates
- Basis of Estimates
- Project Documents Updates

*Question:* **What are the sequence of events the develop schedule process follows?**

- Identify the planned start and finish dates for each activity.
- Have staff review their assigned activities and check for resource calendar conflicts.
- Look for conflicts with activity relationships and level resources if needed.
- Approve and baseline.
- Revise and maintain throughout the project.

*Question:* **What process category does the Develop Schedule process belong to?**

Throughout the project.

*Question:* **What are the inputs to the Develop Schedule process?**

- Project Management Plan
- Project Documents
- Agreements
- EEFs
- OPAs

*Question:* **What are the tools and techniques for the Develop Schedule process?**

- Schedule Network Analysis
- Critical Path Method
- Resource Optimization
- Data Analysis
- Leads and Lags
- Schedule Compression
- Project Management Information System (PMIS)
- Agile Release Planning

*Question:* **What are the outputs of the Develop Schedule process?**

- Project Calendars
- Project Schedule
- Schedule Baseline
- Schedule Data
- Change Requests
- Project Management Plan Updates
- Project Documents Updates

---

*Question:* **What process category does the Control Schedule process belong to?**

Throughout the project.

---

*Question:* **What are the inputs to the Control Schedule process?**

- Project Management Plan
- Project Documents
- Work Performance Data
- OPAs

---

*Question:* **What are the tools and techniques for the Control Schedule process?**

- Data Analysis
- Project Management Information System (PMIS)
- Critical Path Method
- Resource Optimization
- Schedule Compression
- Leads and Lags

---

*Question:* **What are the outputs of the Control Schedule process?**

- Change Requests
- Project Document Updates
- Project Management Plan Updates
- Work Performance Information
- Schedule Forecasts

---

# Chapter 17: Project Cost Management

*Question:* **What are the 4 processes for the project cost management knowledge area?**

- Plan Cost Management
- Estimate Costs
- Determine Budget
- Control Costs

*Define:* **Plan Cost Management Process**

The project cost management process that defines how costs will be estimated, budgeted and controlled.

*Define:* **Estimate Costs Process**

The project cost management process that estimates the amount of money we will need to complete the project.

*Define:* **Determine Budget Process**

The project cost management process that aggregates all estimated costs and arrives at a single cost baseline.

*Define:* **Control Costs Process**

The project cost management process that  monitors changes to the cost baseline.

*Define:* **Earned schedule (ES)**

A new calculation method that extends EVM by using Actual Time (AT).

*Define:* **Actual time (AT)**

The difference between ES and AT (ES – AT) to see if a project is on-schedule.

*Question:* **What are the 5 areas in which Project Cost Management can be tailored?**

- Knowledge management
- Estimating and budgeting
- Earned value management
- Use of agile approach
- Governance

*Define:* **Cost Aggregation**

The act of adding up the costs of work packages, which are then rolled up into higher-level WBS components (such as control accounts) until we come up with a single cost for the entire project.

*Define:* **Cost Baseline**

The approved version of a time-phased project budget that includes contingency reserves but not management reserves.

*Question:* **What is the overall process to calculate the cost baseline?**

- Add up all cost estimates (including contingency reserves) into a work package.
- Add up all work package costs into control accounts.
- Add up all control accounts into a single cost baseline.
- Since costs are tied to scheduled activities, create a view of costs over time.

*Define:* **Cost Estimates**

Coming up with a money amount required to complete the project, as well as contingency reserves for risks, and management reserves to cover unplanned work.

*Define:* **Cost Forecasts**

Achieved when we have either a calculated EAC value or a bottom-up EAC value, which is documented and communicated to stakeholders.

*Define:* **Cost Management Plan**

Describes how costs will be planned, structured and controlled.

*Question:* **What are the 8 areas that are documented in the cost management plan?**

- Units of measure
- Level of precision
- Level of accuracy
- Organizational procedures link
- Control thresholds
- Rules of performance measurement
- Reporting formats
- Additional details

*Define:* **Level of precision**

The degree to which costs will be rounded up or down.

*Define:* **Level of accuracy**

The acceptable range of accuracy used to determine realistic costs.

*Define:* **Organizational procedures link**

Unique numbers assigned to control accounts within the WBS, which are then linked to the organization's accounting system.

*Define:* **Financing**

The act of acquiring funding coming from outside sources.

*Define:* **Funding Limit Reconciliation**

The act of comparing allocated funds against estimated costs, and then somehow bringing them in-line.

*Define:* **Historical Information Review**

Reviewing historical information such as project characteristics, or parameters to calculate parametric or analogous estimates.

*Define:* **Project Funding Requirements**

Ensuring that the overall funding required for a project, as well as periodic funding is calculated from the cost baseline.

---

*Define:* **What process category does the Plan Cost Management process belong to?**

Once or at predefined points.

---

*Question:* **What are the inputs to the Plan Cost Management process?**

- Project Charter
- Project Management Plan
- EEFs
- OPAs

---

*Question:* **What are the tools and techniques for the Plan Cost Management process?**

- Expert Judgement
- Data Analysis
- Meetings

---

*Question:* **What are the outputs of the Plan Cost Management process?**

- Cost Management Plan

---

*Question:* **What process category does the Estimate Costs process belong to?**

Throughout the project.

---

*Question:* **What are the inputs to the Estimate Costs process?**

- Project Management Plan
- Project Documents
- EEFs
- OPAs

---

*Question:* **What are the tools and techniques for the Estimate Costs process?**

- Expert Judgement
- Analogous Estimating
- Parametric Estimating
- Bottom-Up Estimating
- Three-Point Estimating
- Data Analysis
- Project Management Information System (PMIS)
- Decision Making

---

*Question:* **What are the outputs of the Estimate Costs process?**

- Cost Estimates
- Basis of Estimates
- Project Documents Updates

---

*Question:* **What process category does the Determine Budget process belong to?**

Once or at predefined points.

---

*Question:* **What are the inputs to the Determine Budget process?**

- Project Management Plan
- Project Documents
- Business Documents
- Agreements
- EEFs
- OPAs

---

*Question:* **What are the tools and techniques for the Determine Budget process?**

- Expert Judgement
- Cost Aggregation
- Data Analysis
- Historical Information Review
- Funding Limit Reconciliation
- Financing

---

*Question:* **What are the outputs of the Determine Budget process?**

- Cost Baseline
- Project Funding Requirements
- Project Documents Updates

---

*Question:* **What process category does the Control Costs process belong to?**

Throughout the project.

---

*Question:* **What are the inputs to the Control Costs process?**

- Project Management Plan
- Project Documents
- Project Funding Requirements
- Work Performance Data
- OPAs

---

*Question:* **What are the tools and techniques for the Control Costs process?**

- Expert Judgement
- Data Analysis
- To-Complete Performance Index (TCPI)
- Project Management Information System (PMIS)

---

*Question:* **What are the outputs of the Control Costs process?**

- Work Performance Information
- Cost Forecasts
- Change Requests
- Project Management Plan Updates
- Project Documents Updates

---

# Chapter 18: Project Quality Management

*Question:* **What are the 3 processes for the project quality management knowledge area?**

- Plan Quality Management
- Manage Quality
- Control Quality

*Define:* **Plan Quality Management Process**

The project quality management process where we identify quality requirements or standards, and document how we will meet them.

*Define:* **Manage Quality Process**

The project quality management process where we translate the quality management plan into activities that implement our quality plan.

*Define:* **Control Quality Process**

The project quality management process where we see how well we have done to-date on meeting quality standards.

*Define:* **Quality**

A measure of how well the deliverable meets requirements.

*Define:* **Grade**

A category assigned to deliverables having the same functional use but different characteristics.

*Define:* **Prevention**

The act of keeping errors out of the process.

*Define:* **Inspection**

The act of keeping errors out of the hands of the customer.

*Define:* **Attribute sampling**

A decision if a result conforms to the expected value.

*Define:* **Variable sampling**

A measurement of the degree of conformity.

*Define:* **Tolerances**

A range of acceptable results.

*Define:* **Control limits**

The boundaries of commonly-encountered variations.

*Question:* **What are the 5 levels of increasingly effective quality management?**

- Let the customer find the defect.
- Find the defect ourselves before the product is delivered.
- Find the cause of defects and fix the process.
- Put quality into the planning and design.
- Create a culture that is committed to quality throughout.

---

*Question:* **What are 4 trends in quality management to minimize variation while meeting requirements?**

- Customer satisfaction
- Continual improvement
- Management responsibility
- Mutually beneficial partnership with suppliers

---

*Question:* **What are 4 ways in which we can tailor the Project Quality Management knowledge area?**

- Policy compliance and auditing
- Standards and regulatory compliance
- Continuous improvement
- Stakeholder engagement

---

*Define:* **Audits**

A structured process that determines if an activity complies with some policy.

---

*Define:* **Design for X (DfX)**

A set of technical guidelines used during product design to improve the final deliverable.

---

*Define:* **Problem Solving**

The act of finding one or more solutions for an issue.

---

*Question:* **What are the 6 steps involved with problem solving?**

- Identify the problem
- Define the problem
- Investigate
- Analyze
- Solve
- Check the solution

---

*Define:* **Quality Control Measurements**

The documented results of Control Quality activities, and are captured in the format as specified by the quality management plan.

---

*Question:* **What are the 2 most common quality improvement methods?**

- plan-do-check-act (PDCA)
- Six Sigma

---

*Define:* **Quality Management Plan**

A document describing how policies and procedures will result in a quality deliverable, by specifying the needed resources and activities.

---

81

*Define:* **Quality Metrics**

A link from a project or product attribute to the Quality Control process.

---

*Define:* **Quality Reports**

Graphical, numerical or qualitative reports used by processes and departments to achieve quality.

---

*Define:* **Test and Evaluation Documents**

Inputs into the Quality Control process and are used to decide if we have achieved quality.

---

*Define:* **Test and Inspection Planning**

Determining how to test or inspect the deliverable against two standards – the stakeholder's expectations, and against performance and reliability goals.

---

*Define:* **Testing/Product Evaluations**

The act of finding errors or non-conformance problems in the deliverable.

---

*Question:* **What process category does the Plan Quality Management process belong to?**

Once or at predefined points.

---

*Question:* **What are the inputs to the Plan Quality Management process?**

- Project Charter
- Project Management Plan
- Project Documents
- EEFs
- OPAs

---

*Question:* **What are the tools and techniques for the Plan Quality Management process?**

- Expert Judgement
- Data Gathering
- Data Analysis
- Decision Making
- Data Representation
- Test and Inspection Planning
- Meetings

---

*Question:* **What are the outputs for the Plan Quality Management process?**

- Quality Management Plan
- Quality Metrics
- Project Management Plan Updates
- Project Documents Updates

---

*Question:* **What process category does the Manage Quality process belong to?**

Throughout the project.

---

*Question:* **What are the inputs to the Manage Quality process?**

- Project Management Plan
- Project Documents
- OPAs

*Question:* **What are the tools and techniques for the Manage Quality process?**

- Data Gathering
- Data Analysis
- Decision Making
- Data Representation
- Audits
- Design for X
- Problem Solving
- Quality Improvement Methods

*Question:* **What are the outputs for the Manage Quality process?**

- Quality Reports
- Test and Evaluation Documents
- Change Requests
- Project Management Plan Updates
- Project Documents Updates

*Question:* **What process category does the Control Quality process belong to?**

Throughout the project.

*Question:* **What are the inputs to the Control Quality process?**

- Project Management Plan
- Project Documents
- Approved Change Requests
- Deliverables
- Work Performance Data
- EEFs
- OPAs

*Question:* **What are the tools and techniques for the Control Quality process?**

- Data Gathering
- Data Analysis
- Inspection
- Testing/Product Evaluations
- Data Representation
- Meetings

*Question:* **What are the outputs of the Control Quality process?**

- Quality Control Measurements
- Verified Deliverables
- Work Performance Information
- Change Requests
- Project Management Plan Updates
- Project Documents Updates

# Chapter 19: Project Resource Management

*Question:* **What are the 6 processes for the project resource management knowledge area?**

- Plan Resource Management
- Estimate Activity Resources
- Acquire Resources
- Develop Team
- Manage Team
- Control Resources

*Define:* **Plan Resource Management Process**

The project resource management process where we define how to estimate and manage physical and team resources.

*Define:* **Estimate Activity Resources Process**

The project resource management process where we estimate team resources.

*Define:* **Acquire Resources Process**

The project resource management process where we obtain the required resources.

*Define:* **Develop Team Process**

The project resource management process where we improve team competencies, interaction and environment to help achieve the project goals better.

*Define:* **Manage Team Process**

The project resource management process where we track and manage team member performance.

*Define:* **Control Resources Process**

The project resource management process where we ensure physical resources are available when they are needed.

*Define:* **Project team**

Individuals with assigned roles and responsibilities who work collectively to achieve a shared project goal.

*Question:* **What are the 4 ways in which we can tailor the project resource management knowledge area?**

- Resource management methods
- Emotional intelligence (EI)
- Self-organizing teams
- Virtual/distributed teams

*Define:* **Emotional intelligence (EI)**

The awareness and skill of being self-managing and developing relationships, resulting in an emotionally competent group.

*Define:* **Self-organizing teams**

An agile-centric approach in which teams function without any type of central control.

*Define:* **Virtual/distributed teams**

Teams that are not physically located at the same site.

---

*Define:* **Colocation**

Occurs when most team members work from the same physical location.

---

*Define:* **Communication Technology**

Technology such as shared portals, video conferencing, audio conferencing, email or chat.

---

*Question:* **What are some factors that can affect the technology we choose to use?**

- Urgency for the need for information
- Availability and reliability of technology
- Ease of use
- Project environment
- Sensitivity and confidentiality of the information

---

*Define:* **Individual and Team Assessments**

Tools giving the project manager insight into areas of strengths and weaknesses.

---

*Define:* **Organizational Theory**

An examination of the ways in which people and teams behave that can decrease time, cost and effort required for a successful project

---

*Define:* **Physical Resource Assignments**

The documentation of material, equipment, supplies, locations and physical resources to be used during a project.

---

*Define:* **Pre-Assignment**

Occurs when we determine physical or team resources in advance.

---

*Define:* **Project Team Assignments**

Occur when we record team members and their roles and responsibilities.

---

*Define:* **Recognition and Rewards**

A method of successfully developing a team by recognizing and rewarding desirable behavior.

---

*Define:* **Resource Breakdown Structure**

A hierarchy of resources grouped by category and type.

---

*Define:* **Resource Calendars**

Identifies the working days, shifts, start and stop hours and public holidays when a specific resource is (or is not) available.

---

*Define:* **Resource Management Plan**

Tells us how to categorize, allocate and release both human and physical resources.

---

*Question:* **What are the 9 tools used within the resource management plan?**

- Identification of resources
- Acquiring resources
- Roles and responsibilities
- Project organization charts
- Project team resource management
- Training
- Team development
- Resource control
- Recognition plan

*Question:* **What 4 things are identified by roles and responsibilities?**

- Roles
- Authority
- Responsibility
- Competence

*Define:* **Role**

The function assumed by, or assigned to, a person.

*Define:* **Authority**

The right to make decisions and carry out actions to complete an objective.

*Define:* **Responsibility**

The assigned duty or work a team member is expected to complete.

*Define:* **Competence**

The skill and capacity required to complete responsibilities.

*Define:* **Project organization charts**

Graphic displays of team members and their reporting relationships.

*Define:* **Project team resource management**

The act of deciding how team resources should be staffed, managed and released.

*Define:* **Training (within the resource management plan)**

Strategies for training team members.

*Define:* **Team development**

Strategies for developing the project team.

*Define:* **Resource control**

The plan on how we will ensure physical resources are available.

*Define:* **Recognition plan**

The plan on how we will recognize and reward team members for their respective accomplishments.

---

*Define:* **Resource Requirements**

Identifying the types and quantities of resources the project requires.

---

*Define:* **Team Charter**

A document containing clear expectations on team member behavior.

---

*Define:* **Team Performance Assessments**

The act of formally and informally evaluating a team's effectiveness.

---

*Define:* **Training**

All formal and informal activities designed to increase the competencies of team members.

---

*Define:* **Virtual Teams**

A group of people with a shared goal who spend little to no time meeting face-to-face.

---

*Define:* **Resource planning**

The act of identifying an approach to how we will ensure sufficient resources are available so the project will be successful.

---

*Define:* **What process category does the Plan Resource Management process belong to?**

Once or at predefined points.

---

*Question:* **What are the inputs to the Plan Resource Management process?**

- Project Charter
- Project Management Plan
- Project Documents
- EEFs
- OPAs

---

*Question:* **What are the tools and techniques for the Plan Resource Management process?**

- Expert Judgement
- Data Representation
- Organizational Theory
- Meetings

---

*Question:* **What are the outputs of the Plan Resource Management process?**

- Resource Management Plan
- Team Charter
- Project Documents Updates

---

*Question:* **What process category does the Estimate Activity Resources process belong to?**

Throughout the project.

---

*Question:* **What are the inputs to the Estimate Activity Resources process?**

- Project Management Plan
- Project Documents
- EEFs
- OPAs

*Question:* **What are the tools and techniques for the Estimate Activity Resources process?**

- Expert Judgement
- Bottom-Up Estimating
- Analogous Estimating
- Parametric Estimating
- Data Analysis
- Project Management Information System (PMIS)
- Meetings

*Question:* **What are the outputs of the Estimate Activity Resources process?**

- Resource Requirements
- Basis of Estimates
- Resource Breakdown Structure
- Project Documents Updates

*Question:* **What process category does the Acquire Resources process belong to?**

Throughout the project.

*Question:* **What are the inputs to the Acquire Resources process?**

- Project Management Plan
- Project Documents
- EEFs
- OPAs

*Question:* **What are the tools and techniques for the Acquire Resources process?**

- Decision Making
- Interpersonal and Team Skills
- Pre-Assignment
- Virtual Teams

*Question:* **What are the outputs of the Acquire Resources process?**

- Physical Resource Assignments
- Project Team Assignments
- Resource Calendars
- Change Requests
- Project Management Plan Updates
- Project Documents Updates
- EEFs
- OPAs

*Define:* **Tuckman ladder**

A 'develop team' model that outlines 5 stages of development that teams go through.

*Question:* **What are the 5 stages of development the Tuckman Ladder lists?**

- Forming
- Storming
- Norming
- Performing
- Adjourning

*Question:* **What process category does the Develop Team process belong to?**

Throughout the project.

*Question:* **What are the inputs to the Develop Team process?**

- Project Management Plan
- Project Documents
- EEFs
- OPAs

*Question:* **What are the tools and techniques for the Develop Team process?**

- Colocation
- Virtual Teams
- Communication Technology
- Interpersonal and Team Skills
- Recognition and Rewards
- Training
- Individual and Team Assessments
- Meetings

*Question:* **What are the outputs of the Develop Team process?**

- Team Performance Assessments
- Change Requests
- Project Management Plan Updates
- Project Documents Updates
- EEFs
- OPAs

*Question:* **What process category does the Manage Team process belong to?**

Throughout the project.

*Question:* **What are the inputs to the Manage Team process?**

- Project Management Plan
- Project Documents
- Work Performance Reports
- Team Performance Assessments
- EEFs
- OPAs

*Question:* **What are the tools and techniques for the Manage Team process?**

- Interpersonal and Team Skills
- Project Management Information System (PMIS)

*Question:* **What are the outputs of the Manage Team process?**

- Change Requests
- Project Management Plan Updates
- Project Documents Updates
- EEFs

*Question:* **What process category does the Control Resources process belong to?**

Throughout the project.

*Question:* **What are the inputs to the Control Resources process?**

- Project Management Plan
- Project Documents
- Work Performance Data
- Agreements
- OPAs

*Question:* **What are the tools and techniques for the Control Resources process?**

- Data Analysis
- Problem Solving
- Interpersonal and Team Skills
- Project Management Information System (PMIS)

*Question:* **What are the outputs of the Control Resources process?**

- Work Performance Information
- Change Requests
- Project Management Plan Updates
- Project Documents Updates

# Chapter 20: Project Communications Management

*Question:* **What are the 3 processes for the project communications management knowledge area?**

- Plan Communications Management
- Manage Communications
- Monitor Communications

*Define:* **Plan Communications Management Process**

A project communications management process where we figure out how we will communicate between the project and stakeholders.

*Define:* **Manage Communications Process**

A project communications management process in which we collect and distribute information to the right audience at the right time.

*Define:* **Monitor Communications Process**

A project communications management process where we watch communication as it happens and make sure it follows the plan.

*Define:* **Communication**

The exchange of voluntary or involuntary information in the form of ideas, instructions or emotions.

*Question:* **What are the 6 mechanisms through which we communicate?**

- Written
- Spoken
- Formal or informal
- Gestures
- Media
- Choice of words

*Question:* **What are the 5 dimensions of communication activities?**

- Internal vs. external
- Formal vs. informal
- Hierarchical focus
- Official vs. unofficial
- Written vs. oral

*Question:* **What are the 3 dimensions of hierarchical focus communication?**

- Upward
- Downward
- Horizontal

*Question:* **What are the _5Cs_ of written communication?**

- **Correct** grammar and spelling
- **Concise** expression and elimination of excess words
- **Clear** purpose and expressions directed to the needs of the reader.
- **Coherent** logical flow of ideas by using 'markers' such as introductions and summaries.
- **Controlling** flow of words and ideas by using graphics or summaries.

*Question:* **What are some trends for project communications management?**

- Inclusion of stakeholders in project reviews
- Inclusion of stakeholders in project meetings
- Increased use of social computing
- Multifaceted approaches to communication

*Question:* **What possibilities are there for tailoring project communications management?**

- Stakeholders
- Physical location
- Communications technology
- Language
- Knowledge management

*Question:* **What are the 4 aspects of communication skills?**

- Active listening
- Being aware of cultural and personal differences
- Identifying, setting and managing stakeholder expectations
- Enhancement of team member skills

*Define:* **Communication Methods**

A technique allowing us to share information.

*Question:* **What are the 3 communication method classifications?**

- Interactive communication
- Push communication
- Pull communication

*Define:* **Interactive communication**

Communication happening in real-time.

*Define:* **Push communication**

Communication occurring when we send information out to specific recipients but do not check to see if it was received or understood.

*Define:* **Pull communication**

Communication occurring when we place information on a portal or other shared platform, and individuals or groups access the information as they see the need to.

*Question:* **What are the 5 different forms of communication?**

- Interpersonal communication
- Small group communication
- Public communication
- Mass communication
- Networks and social computing communication

*Define:* **Interpersonal communication**

Information exchanged between individuals, typically face-to-face.

*Define:* **Small group communication**

Communication occurring in groups of 3 to 6 people.

*Define:* **Public communication**

Communication when a speaker addresses a group of people.

*Define:* **Mass communication**

Communication represented by a minimal connection between the sender and a large, anonymous audience.

*Define:* **Networks and social computing communication**

Communication of many-to-many.

*Define:* **Communication Management Plan**

A subset of the project management plan that contains guidelines and templates for status meetings, team meetings, e-meetings and email messages.

*Question:* **What are the 2 forms of the communication process?**

- Sample basic sender/receiver communication model
- Sample interactive communication model

*Question:* **What are the 3 steps in the sample basic sender/receiver communication model?**

- Encode
- Transmit
- Decode

*Question:* **What are the 5 steps in the sample interactive communication model?**

- Encode
- Transmit
- Decode
- Acknowledge
- Feedback/Response

*Define:* **Emotional state**

All the influences that affect how messages are created, sent and understood.

*Define:* **Communication Requirements Analysis**

An analysis technique used to determine the information needs of stakeholders, and is done by combining the type and format of information needed with the value of that information.

*Define:* **Communication competence**

The possession of skills such as providing clarity of purpose in key messages, effective relationships and leadership behaviors.

*Define:* **Feedback**

The ability to coach, mentor and negotiate.

*Define:* **Nonverbal**

The act of transmitting the proper meaning through gestures, tone of voice and facial expressions.

*Define:* **Presentations**

The formal delivery of information.

*Define:* **Project Communications**

Artifacts including reports, deliverable statuses, schedule progress and presentations.

*Define:* **Project Reporting**

The act of collecting and distributing project information.

*Define:* **Communications management plan**

A document detailing how we will present relevant information in a timely manner so that stakeholders remain engaged.

*Question:* **What process category does the Plan Communications Management process belong to?**

Throughout the project.

*Question:* **What are the inputs to the Plan Communications Management process?**

- Project Charter
- Project Management Plan
- Project Documents
- EEFs
- OPAs

*Question:* **What are the tools and techniques for the Plan Communications Management process?**

- Expert Judgement
- Communication Requirements Analysis
- Communication Technology
- Communication Models
- Communication Methods
- Interpersonal and Team Skills
- Data Representation
- Meetings

*Question:* **What are the outputs of the Plan Communications Management process?**

- Communication Management Plan
- Project Management Plan Updates
- Project Documents Updates

*Question:* **What 7 techniques should we take into consideration for the manage communications process?**

- Sender-receiver models
- Choice of media
- Writing style
- Meeting management
- Presentations
- Facilitation
- Active listening

*Question:* **What process category does the Manage Communications process belong to?**

Throughout the project.

*Question:* **What are the inputs to the Manage Communications process?**

- Project Management Plan
- Project Documents
- Work Performance Reports
- EEFs
- OPAs

*Question:* **What are the tools and techniques for the Manage Communications process?**

- Communication Technology
- Communication Methods
- Communication Skills
- Project Management Information System (PMIS)
- Project Reporting
- Interpersonal and Team Skills
- Meetings

*Question:* **What are the outputs of the Manage Communications process?**

- Project Communications
- Project Management Plan Updates
- Project Documents Updates
- OPAs

*Question:* **What process category does the Monitor Communications process belong to?**

Throughout the project.

*Question:* **What are the inputs to the Monitor Communications process?**

- Project Management Plan
- Project Documents
- Work Performance Data
- EEFs
- OPAs

*Question:* **What are the tools and techniques for the Monitor Communications process?**

- Expert Judgement
- Project Management Information System (PMIS)
- Data Representation
- Interpersonal and Team Skills
- Meetings

*Question:* **What are the outputs of the Monitor Communications process?**
- Work Performance Information
- Change Requests
- Project Management Plan Updates
- Project Documents Updates

# Chapter 21: Project Risk Management

*Question:* **What are the 7 processes for the project risk management knowledge area?**

- Plan Risk Management
- Identify Risks
- Perform Qualitative Risk Analysis
- Perform Quantitative Risk Analysis
- Plan Risk Responses
- Implement Risk Responses
- Monitor Risks

*Define:* **Plan Risk Management Process**

A project risk management process where we decide how we are going to conduct risk management.

*Define:* **Identify Risks Process**

A project risk management process where we identify and document individual and overall project risks.

*Define:* **Perform Qualitative Risk Analysis Process**

A project risk management process where we prioritize risks for further analysis according to probability of occurrence.

*Define:* **Perform Quantitative Risk Analysis Process**

A project risk management process where we assign a numerical value to risks.

*Define:* **Plan Risk Responses Process**

A project risk management process where we decide how to address individual and overall risk exposure.

*Define:* **Implement Risk Responses Process**

A project risk management process where we implement the risk plan.

*Question:* **What are the 2 types of risk?**

- Individual project risk
- Overall project risk

*Define:* **Individual project risk**

An uncertain event or condition.

*Define:* **Overall project risk**

The effect of individual project risk uncertainty on the project as a whole.

*Define:* **Positive risk**

A risk that we will not take advantage of an opportunity.

*Define:* **Negative risk**

An unmanaged threat that could result in things like delay, cost overruns or performance shortfalls.

*Define:* **Emergent risks**

Risk appearing after the project initiation.

*Define:* **Risk threshold**

A measurable value that reflects our appetite for accepting that risk.

*Define:* **Non-event risk**

A risk that does not arise out of an event.

*Define:* **Variability risk**

Encountered when we are not confident about a characteristic of some event, activity or decision.

*Define:* **Ambiguity risks**

Encountered when we are uncertain about what will happen in the future.

*Define:* **Unknowable-unknowns**

Things we don't and can't know about until we encounter them.

*Define:* **Project resilience**

How we tackle emergent risks.

*Define:* **Integrated risk management**

The act of addressing risks at every level in the same manner.

*Question:* **What are 4 tailoring considerations for the project risk management knowledge area?**

- Project size
- Project complexity
- Project importance
- Development approach

*Define:* **Contingent Response Strategies**

A response that is used only if a specific event happens.

*Define:* **Contingency plans**

Also called fallback plans, documentation on executing a relevant plan when a specific pre-planned risk is encountered.

*Define:* **Prompt Lists**

A predefined list of categories representing individual project risks used as an aid to 'prompt' team members when generating a list of risks to the project.

*Question:* **What are 3 common prompt list frameworks?**

- PESTLE (political, economic, social, technological, legal, environmental)
- TECOP (technical, environmental, commercial, operational, political)
- VUCA (volatility, uncertainty, complexity, ambiguity)

---

*Define:* **Representation of Uncertainty**

Individual project risks and other sources of uncertainty around duration, cost or requirements.

---

*Define:* **Risk Categorization**

The categorization of risks to determine which areas of the project have the most uncertainty.

---

*Define:* **Risk Management Plan**

A document describing how risk management activities will be structured and performed.

---

*Define:* **Risk Strategy**

The general approach to managing risk.

---

*Define:* **Risk Methodology**

The approaches, tools and data sources used to perform risk management.

---

*Define:* **Risk Roles and responsibilities**

A definition of the lead, support and risk management team members for each type of activity, providing clarity on their respective responsibilities.

---

*Define:* **Risk Funding**

An identification of the funds needed for risk management activities, and establishes the protocols for how contingency and management reserves will be applied.

---

*Define:* **Risk Timing**

A definition of when and how often risk management activities will be executed.

---

*Define:* **Risk breakdown structure (RBS)**

A hierarchical representation of potential sources of risk

---

*Define:* **Stakeholder risk appetite**

The measurable risk thresholds around each project goal.

---

*Define:* **Probability and impact matrix**

A grid for mapping the probability of each risk and its impact.

---

*Define:* **Risk Tracking**

The act of recording risk activities and auditing risk management processes.

---

*Define:* **Risk Register**

A repository capturing the details for identified individual project risks.

*Question:* **What are the 3 components of the risk register?**

- List of Identified Risks
- Potential Risk Owners
- List of Potential Risk Responses

*Define:* **Risk Report**

A report presenting overall project risks, and includes a summary of individual risks.

*Define:* **Strategies for Opportunities**

The act of defining how we will deal with opportunities we want to take advantage of.

*Question:* **What are the five strategies to deal with opportunities?**

- Escalate
- Exploit
- Share
- Enhance
- Accept

*Define:* **Opportunity Escalation**

Occurs when an opportunity is passed on to someone outside of the project.

*Define:* **Opportunity Exploitation**

Making sure the probability of occurrence reaches 100%

*Define:* **Opportunity Sharing**

Transferring ownership of the opportunity to a third-party so that it shares in the benefit.

*Define:* **Opportunity Enhancement**

Occurs when we increase the probability and/or impact of the opportunity.

*Define:* **Opportunity Acceptance**

Occurs when we acknowledge the opportunity, but purposefully decide to take no action.

*Define:* **Active Opportunity Acceptance**

Occurs when we accept the opportunity by creating a contingency reserve in case it occurs.

*Define:* **Passive Opportunity Acceptance**

The act of taking no further action other than monitoring an opportunity in case it changes.

*Define:* **Strategies for Threats**

The various ways in which we will deal with a threat we want to avoid.

---

*Question:* **What are the five strategies to deal with threats?**

- Escalate
- Avoid
- Transfer
- Mitigate
- Accept

---

*Define:* **Threat Escalation**

Occurs when a threat is escalated above the project level.

---

*Define:* **Threat Avoidance**

Happens when we eliminate the threat or protect the project from its impact.

---

*Define:* **Threat Transfer**

Results when we shift ownership of a threat to a third party who bears the impact if the threat occurs.

---

*Define:* **Threat Mitigation**

Occurs when we act to reduce the likelihood of occurrence and/or impact.

---

*Define:* **Threat Acceptance**

Happens when we acknowledge the threat, but purposefully decide to take no action.

---

*Define:* **Active Threat Acceptance**

The act of accepting a risk by creating a contingency reserve.

---

*Define:* **Passive Threat Acceptance**

The act of taking no further action other than monitoring a risk in case it changes.

---

*Question:* **What are the 5 strategies for overall project risk?**

- Avoid
- Exploit
- Transfer/share
- Mitigate/enhance
- Accept

---

*Question:* **What process category does the Plan Risk Management process belong to?**

Once or at predefined points.

---

*Question:* **What are the inputs to the Plan Risk Management process?**

- Project Charter
- Project Management Plan
- Project Documents
- EEFs
- OPAs

*Question:* **What are the tools and techniques for the Plan Risk Management process?**

- Expert Judgement
- Data Analysis
- Meetings

*Question:* **What are the outputs of the Plan Risk Management process?**

- Risk Management Plan

*Question:* **What process category does the Identify Risks process belong to?**

Throughout the project.

*Question:* **What are the inputs to the Identify Risks process?**

- Project Management Plan
- Project Documents Management
- Agreements
- Procurement Documentation
- EEFs
- OPAs

*Question:* **What are the tools and techniques for the Identify Risks process?**

- Expert Judgement
- Data Gathering
- Data Analysis
- Interpersonal and Team Skills
- Prompt Lists
- Meetings

*Question:* **What are the outputs of the Identify Risks process?**

- Risk Register
- Risk Report
- Project Documents Updates

*Question:* **What process category does the Perform Qualitative Risk Analysis process belong to?**

Throughout the project.

*Question:* **What are the inputs to the Perform Qualitative Risk Analysis process?**

- Project Management Plan
- Project Documents
- EEFs
- OPAs

*Question:* **What are the tools and techniques for the Perform Qualitative Risk Analysis process?**

- Expert Judgement
- Data Gathering
- Data Analysis
- Interpersonal and Team Skills
- Risk Categorization
- Data Representation
- Meetings

---

*Question:* **What are the outputs of the Perform Qualitative Risk Analysis process?**

- Project Documents Updates

---

*Question:* **What process category does the Perform Quantitative Risk Analysis process belong to?**

Throughout the project (when the project requires it).

---

*Question:* **What are the inputs to the Perform Quantitative Risk Analysis process?**

- Project Management Plan
- Project Documents
- EEFs
- OPAs

---

*Question:* **What are the tools and techniques for the Perform Quantitative Risk Analysis process?**

- Expert Judgement
- Data Gathering
- Interpersonal and Team Skills
- Representation of Uncertainty
- Data Analysis

---

*Question:* **What are the outputs of the Perform Quantitative Risk Analysis process?**

- Project Documents Updates

---

*Define:* **Risk owner**

A person nominated for the job of implementing a risk plan.

---

*Define:* **Secondary risks**

Risks that arise as a direct result of implementing a risk response.

---

*Question:* **What process category does the Plan Risk Responses process belong to?**

Throughout the project.

---

*Question:* **What are the inputs to the Plan Risk Responses process?**

- Project Management Plan
- Project Documents
- EEFs
- OPAs

*Question:* **What are the tools and techniques for the Plan Risk Responses process?**

- Expert Judgement
- Data Gathering
- Interpersonal and Team Skills
- Strategies for Threats
- Strategies for Opportunities
- Contingent Response Strategies
- Strategies for Overall Project Risk
- Data Analysis
- Decision Making

*Question:* **What are the outputs of the Plan Risk Responses process?**

- Change Requests
- Project Management Plan Updates
- Project Documents Updates

*Question:* **What process category does the Implement Risk Responses process belong to?**

Throughout the project.

*Question:* **What are the inputs to the Implement Risk Responses process?**

- Project Management Plan
- Project Documents
- OPAs

*Question:* **What are the tools and techniques for the Implement Risk Responses process?**

- Expert Judgement
- Interpersonal and Team Skills
- Project Management Information System (PMIS)

*Question:* **What are the outputs of the Implement Risk Responses process?**

- Change Requests
- Project Documents Updates

*Question:* **What process category does the Monitor Risks process belong to?**

Throughout the project.

*Question:* **What are the inputs to the Monitor Risks process?**

- Project Management Plan
- Project Documents
- Work Performance Data
- Work Performance Reports

*Question:* **What are the tools and techniques for the Monitor Risks process?**

- Data Analysis
- Audits
- Meetings

104

*Question:* **What are the outputs of the Monitor Risks process?**

- Work Performance Information
- Change Requests
- Project Management Plan Updates
- Project Documents Updates
- Organizational Process Assets Updates

# Chapter 22: Project Procurement Management

*Question:* **What are the 3 processes in the project procurement management knowledge area?**

- Plan Procurement Management
- Conduct Procurements
- Control Procurements

*Define:* **Plan Procurement Management Process**

The project procurement management process where we document procurement decisions such as the approach and sellers.

*Define:* **Conduct Procurements Process**

The project procurement management process where we obtain seller responses, select a seller and award a contract.

*Define:* **Control Procurements Process**

The project procurement management process where we manage seller relationships, monitor performance according to the contract, make changes as needed and close the contract out.

*Question:* **What are the 5 forms an agreement can take?**

- Contract
- Service Level Agreement (SLA)
- Understanding
- Memorandum of Agreement (MOA)
- Purchase order

*Question:* **What are the 6 trends to watch for in the project procurement management knowledge area?**

- Advances in tools
- More advanced risk management
- Changing contract processes
- Logistics and supply chain management
- Technology or stakeholder relations
- Trial engagement

*Question:* **What are 2 reasons that webcams at construction sites are now the norm?**

- It increases visibility into progress for stakeholders
- It provides a permanent record over time of activities at the site in case there are disputes later

*Question:* **What are 2 reasons why we might want to source supplies from multiple, competing vendors?**

- Evaluate products from each vendor and select the best choice
- Continue making progress on the project before the selection is finalized

*Question:* **What are 4 tailoring considerations for the project procurement management knowledge area?**

- Complexity of procurement
- Physical location
- Governance and regulatory environment
- Availability of contractors

*Define:* **Master services agreement (MSA)**

An agreement in which adaptive work is placed into a contract appendix, allowing changes to happen on the adaptive scope without impacting the overall contract.

---

*Define:* **Advertising**

The act of communicating with potential sellers about a product or service.

---

*Define:* **Bid Documents**

A document used to solicit proposals from potential sellers.

---

*Question:* **What are the 3 types of bid documents?**

- Request for information (RFI)
- Request for quotation (RFQ)
- Request for proposal (RFP)

---

*Define:* **Request for information (RFI)**

A bid document which requests information on goods or services before an RFQ or RFP is issued.

---

*Define:* **Request for quotation (RFQ)**

A bid document which requests information on how a vendor would satisfy requirements.

---

*Define:* **Request for proposal (RFP)**

A bid document which is used when there is a problem in the project and we are unsure of a solution.

---

*Define:* **Bidder Conferences**

A meeting between the buyer and prospective sellers prior to submitting a proposal.

---

*Question:* **What are the 2 reasons for bidder conferences?**

- To ensure that all bidders have a clear understanding of the procurement request
- To ensure that no bidders receive preferential treatment.

---

*Define:* **Claims Administration**

The act of handling claims arising from contractual disputes for either party.

---

*Define:* **Claim**

An issue arising when we have real or potential contested changes to the contract, and the two parties cannot reach an agreement that a change has occurred, or on compensation for an agreed upon change.

---

*Define:* **Alternative dispute resolution (ADR)**

A process to handle unresolved claims that is established in a contract.

---

## 107

*Define:* **Closed Procurement**

Results when we officially close out a contract.

---

*Question:* **What 3 things must be true before we can close out a contract?**

- All deliverables have been delivered on-time and meet technical and quality requirements.
- There are no outstanding claims or invoices.
- All final payments have been made.

---

*Define:* **Independent Cost Estimates**

Results when we elect to have an external party prepare cost estimates for us so that we can perform a sanity check against potential vendor estimates.

---

*Define:* **Make-or-Buy Decisions**

An act that informs us if work is best suited for the project team or should be outsourced.

---

*Question:* **What are some procurement documents that might need updating?**

- Schedules
- Unapproved contract changes
- Approved contract change requests
- Seller-developed technical documentation
- Deliverables
- Seller performance reports
- Warranties

---

*Define:* **Procurement Documentation**

A document providing a written record used in reaching legal agreements.

---

*Question:* **What are 4 items included in procurement documentation?**

- Bid documents
- Procurement statement of work
- Independent cost estimates
- Source selection criteria

---

*Define:* **Procurement Management Plan**

A document containing all activities that need to happen during the procurement process, and what kind of bidding should be used.

---

*Define:* **Procurement Statement of Work**

A document describing only the portion of the project that applies to the current procurement process, and should be included in any contract.

---

*Define:* **Terms of reference (TOR)**

A document similar to an SOW, but includes detailed descriptions.

---

*Question:* **What are the 3 things procurement strategy is concerned with?**

- Delivery methods
- Contract payment types
- Procurement phases.

*Question:* **What are the 4 delivery methods for professional services?**

- Buyer/services provider with no subcontracting
- Buyer/services provider with subcontracting allowed
- Joint venture between buyer/seller
- Buyer/services provider acts as the representative

*Question:* **What are the 5 delivery methods for construction projects?**

- Turnkey
- Design build (DB)
- Design bid build (DBB)
- Design build operate (DBO)
- Build, own, operate, transfer (BOOT)

*Define:* **Contract payment types**

How seller payments are coordinated with the buyer's internal financial systems.

*Question:* **What are the 5 items included with procurement phases information?**

- Sequencing
- Milestones
- Criteria for moving to the next phase
- Tracking progress
- How knowledge will be transferred

*Define:* **Selected Sellers**

A vendor that has passed all criteria and has been tentatively approved to receive a signed contract.

*Define:* **Seller Proposals**

The package a seller sends back in response to a request.

*Define:* **Source Selection Analysis**

An analysis technique used to document how potential sellers will be evaluated.

*Question:* **What are the 6 common selection methods used with sellers?**

- Least cost
- Qualifications only
- Quality-based/highest technical proposal
- Quality and cost-based
- Sole source
- Fixed budget

*Define:* **Least cost seller selection method**

A selection method used when the purchased product is of a routine nature.

*Define:* **Qualifications only seller selection method**

A selection method used when the cost of the product is relatively small and the decision is based on the seller's reputation and expertise.

---

*Define:* **Quality-based/highest technical proposal seller selection method**

A selection method in which we evaluate and rank technical solutions from all vendors first, and then evaluate the cost starting with the vendor providing the best technical solution.

---

*Define:* **Quality and cost-based seller selection method**

A selection method used when project risk is relatively high and quality is an absolute must. After quality, cost is considered.

---

*Define:* **Sole source seller selection method**

A selection method used when a single vendor is involved.

---

*Define:* **Fixed budget seller selection method**

A selection method used when no changes are anticipated and the seller knows exactly what budget the project can afford.

---

*Define:* **Source Selection Criteria**

The definition of how we will select the winning vendor.

---

*Define:* **Local content**

A requirement that a set amount of staff must originate from the area local to the vendor.

---

*Define:* **Preapproved seller list**

A document that can streamline the steps needed to advertise to and select the seller.

---

*Define:* **Formal procurement policies, procedures and guidelines**

Existing resources that can relieve the project from the burden of managing the formal procurement process.

---

*Question:* **What are the 3 categories of contract types?**

- Fixed-price
- Cost-reimbursable
- Time and materials

---

*Define:* **Fixed-price contracts**

A contract established by agreeing on a fixed total price for a well-defined deliverable.

---

*Question:* **What are the 3 types of fixed-price contracts?**

- Firm-fixed price (FFP)
- Fixed-price incentive fee (FPIF)
- Fixed-price with economic price adjustments (FPEPA)

---

## 110

*Define:* **Firm-fixed price (FFP)**

The most common type of fixed-price contract because the price is not subject to change unless the scope changes.

---

*Define:* **Fixed-price incentive fee (FPIF)**

A fixed-price contract that gives both parties some flexibility in that it allows for deviation in performance, with financial incentives tied to achieving a certain level of performance.

---

*Define:* **Fixed-price with economic price adjustments (FPEPA)**

A fixed-price contract which is used when the sellers' performance period spans multiple years or if the payments are made in a foreign currency.

---

*Define:* **Cost-reimbursable contracts**

A contract requiring the buyer to reimburse the seller for all costs, plus a fee representing the seller's profit.

---

*Question:* **What are the 3 variations of a cost-reimbursable contract?**

- Cost plus fixed fee (CPFF)
- Cost plus incentive fee (CPIF)
- Cost plus award fee (CPAF)

---

*Define:* **Cost plus fixed fee (CPFF)**

A cost-reimbursable contract where the seller is reimbursed for costs plus a fixed-fee payment based as a percentage of the initial estimated costs.

---

*Define:* **Cost plus incentive fee (CPIF)**

A cost-reimbursable contract where the seller is reimbursed for costs plus a pre-determined incentive fee if certain performance goals are met.

---

*Define:* **Cost plus award fee (CPAF)**

A cost-reimbursable contract where the seller is reimbursed for cost plus a fee based on how well the deliverables meet predefined performance criteria.

---

*Define:* **Time and material contract (T&M)**

A contract that is a hybrid of cost-reimbursable and fixed-price contracts.

---

*Define:* **What process category does the Plan Procurement Management process belong to?**

Once or at predefined points.

---

*Question:* **What are the inputs to the Plan Procurement Management process?**

- Project Charter
- Business Documents
- Project Management Plan
- Project Documents
- EEFs
- OPAs

---

*Question:* **What are the tools and techniques for the Plan Procurement Management process?**

- Expert Judgement
- Data Gathering
- Data Analysis
- Source Selection Analysis
- Meetings

*Question:* **What are the outputs of the Plan Procurement Management process?**

- Procurement Management Plan
- Procurement Strategy
- Bid Documents
- Procurement Statement of Work
- Source Selection Criteria
- Make-or-Buy Decisions
- Independent Cost Estimates
- Change Requests
- Project Documents Updates
- Organizational Process Assets Updates

*Question:* **What process category does the Conduct Procurements process belong to?**

Throughout the project.

*Question:* **What are the inputs to the Conduct Procurements process?**

- Project Management Plan
- Project Documents
- Procurement Documentation
- Seller Proposals
- EEFs
- OPAs

*Question:* **What are the tools and techniques for the Conduct Procurements process?**

- Expert Judgement
- Advertising
- Bidder Conferences
- Data Analysis
- Interpersonal and Team Skills

*Question:* **What are the outputs of the Conduct Procurements process?**

- Selected Sellers
- Agreements
- Change Requests
- Project Management Plan Updates
- Project Documents Updates
- Organizational Process Assets Updates

*Question:* **What process category does the Control Procurements process belong to?**

Throughout the project.

## 112

*Question:* **What are the inputs to the Control Procurements process?**

- Project Management Plan
- Project Documents
- Agreements
- Procurement Documentation
- Approved Change Requests
- Work Performance Data
- EEFs
- OPAs

*Question:* **What are the tools and techniques for the Control Procurements process?**

- Expert Judgement
- Claims Administration
- Data Analysis
- Inspection
- Audits

*Question:* **What are the outputs of the Control Procurements process?**

- Closed Procurements
- Work Performance Information
- Procurement Documentation Updates
- Change Requests
- Project Management Plan Updates
- Project Documents Updates
- Organizational Process Assets Updates

# Chapter 23: Project Stakeholder Management

*Question:* **What are the 4 processes in the project stakeholder management knowledge area?**

- Identify Stakeholders
- Plan Stakeholder Engagement
- Manage Stakeholder Engagement
- Monitor Stakeholder Engagement

*Define:* **Identify Stakeholders Process**

A process in the project stakeholder management knowledge area that names stakeholders and documents relevant details.

*Define:* **Plan Stakeholder Engagement Process**

A process in the project stakeholder management knowledge area that tells us how we will involve stakeholders throughout the project.

*Define:* **Manage Stakeholder Engagement Process**

A process in the project stakeholder management knowledge area where we communicate to stakeholders.

*Define:* **Monitor Stakeholder Engagement Process**

A process in the project stakeholder management knowledge area where we watch stakeholder relationships.

*Question:* **What are the 3 events around which activities in the project stakeholder management knowledge area should be executed?**

- When the project moves from one phase to the next.
- As current stakeholders are no longer involved and new ones join.
- When there are big changes in the organization or the wider stakeholder community.

*Question:* **What are 5 trends to watch for in the project stakeholder management knowledge area?**

- Identifying all stakeholders, not just a limited set.
- Ensuring all team members are involved in stakeholder engagements.
- Reviewing the stakeholder community regularly
- Using co-creation
- Capturing the value of stakeholder engagement

*Define:* **Co-creation**

The act of placing a greater emphasis on including stakeholders as partners.

*Question:* **What are 3 tailoring possibilities in the project stakeholder management knowledge area?**

- Stakeholder diversity
- Complexity of stakeholder relationships
- Communication technology

*Define:* **Ground Rules**

A list of expected stakeholder engagement behaviors for both project teams and stakeholders.

*Define:* **Stakeholder Engagement Plan**

A subset of the project management plan that tells us how we are going to keep stakeholders engaged in decision making and execution.

---

*Define:* **Stakeholder Register**

A document containing information about stakeholders.

---

*Question:* **What 3 items does the stakeholder register include?**

- Identification information
- Assessment information
- Stakeholder classification

---

*Question:* **What process category does the Identify Stakeholders process belong to?**

Throughout the project.

---

*Question:* **What are the inputs to the Identify Stakeholders process?**

- Project Charter
- Business Documents
- Project Management Plan
- Project Documents
- Agreements
- EEFs
- OPAs

---

*Question:* **What are the tools and techniques for the Identify Stakeholders process?**

- Expert Judgement
- Data Gathering
- Data Analysis
- Data Representation
- Meetings

---

*Question:* **What are the outputs of the Identify Stakeholders process?**

- Stakeholder Register
- Change Requests
- Project Management Plan Updates
- Project Documents Updates

---

*Question:* **What process category does the Plan Stakeholder Engagement process belong to?**

Throughout the project.

---

*Question:* **What are the inputs to the Plan Stakeholder Engagement process?**

- Project Charter
- Project Management Plan
- Project Documents
- Agreements
- EEFs
- OPAs

*Question:* **What are the tools and techniques for the Plan Stakeholder Engagement process?**
- Expert Judgement
- Data Gathering
- Data Analysis
- Decision Making
- Data Representation
- Meetings

*Question:* **What are the outputs of the Plan Stakeholder Engagement process?**

- Stakeholder Engagement Plan

*Question:* **What process category does the Manage Stakeholder Engagement process belong to?**

Throughout the project.

*Question:* **What are the inputs to the Manage Stakeholder Engagement process?**

- Project Management Plan
- Project Documents
- EEFs
- OPAs

*Question:* **What are the tools and techniques for the Manage Stakeholder Engagement process?**

- Expert Judgement
- Communication Skills
- Interpersonal and Team Skills
- Ground Rules
- Meetings

*Question:* **What are the outputs of the Manage Stakeholder Engagement process?**

- Change Requests
- Project Management Plan Updates
- Project Documents Updates

*Question:* **What process category does the Monitor Stakeholder Engagement process belong to?**

Throughout the project.

*Question:* **What are the inputs to the Monitor Stakeholder Engagement process?**

- Project Management Plan
- Project Documents
- Work Performance Data
- EEFs
- OPAs

*Question:* **What are the tools and techniques for the Monitor Stakeholder Engagement process?**

- Data Analysis
- Decision Making
- Data Representation
- Communication Skills
- Interpersonal and Team Skills
- Meetings

*Question:* **What are the outputs of the Monitor Stakeholder Engagement process?**

- Work Performance Information
- Change Requests
- Project Management Plan Updates
- Project Documents Updates

# Common Acronyms

*Define:* **AC**

Actual Cost

*Define:* **BAC**

Budget at Completion

*Define:* **CCB**

Change Control Board

*Define:* **COQ**

Cost of Quality

*Define:* **CPAF**

Cost Plus Award Fee

*Define:* **CPFF**

Cost Plus Fixed Fee

*Define:* **CPI**

Cost Performance Index

*Define:* **CPIF**

Cost Plus Incentive Fee

*Define:* **CPM**

Critical Path Method

*Define:* **CV**

Cost Variance

*Define:* **EAC**

Estimate at Completion

*Define:* **EF**

Early Finish Date

# Common Acronyms

*Define:* **ES**

Early Start Date

*Define:* **ETC**

Estimate to Complete

*Define:* **EV**

Earned Value

*Define:* **EVM**

Earned Value Management

*Define:* **FF**

Finish-To-Finish

*Define:* **FFP**

Firm Fixed Price

*Define:* **FPEPA**

Fixed Price with Economic Price Adjustment

*Define:* **FPIF**

Fixed Price Incentive Fee

*Define:* **FS**

Finish to Start

*Define:* **IFB**

Invitation for Bid

*Define:* **LF**

Late Finish Date

*Define:* **LOE**

Level of Effort

*Define:* **LS**

Late Start Date

## 119

*Define:* **OBS**

Organizational Breakdown Structure

*Define:* **PDM**

Precedence Diagramming Method

*Define:* **PMBOK**

Project Management Body of Knowledge

*Define:* **PV**

Planned Value

*Define:* **QFD**

Quality Function Deployment

*Define:* **RACI**

Responsible, Accountable, Consult, And Inform

*Define:* **RAM**

Responsibility Assignment Matrix

*Define:* **RBS**

Risk Breakdown Structure

*Define:* **RFI**

Request for Information

*Define:* **RFP**

Request for Proposal

*Define:* **RFQ**

Request for Quotation

*Define:* **SF**

Start-To-Finish

*Define:* **SOW**

Statement of Work

# Common Acronyms

*Define:* **SPI**

Schedule Performance Index

*Define:* **SV**

Schedule Variance

*Define:* **SWOT**

Strengths, Weaknesses, Opportunities and Threats

*Define:* **T&M**

Time and Material Contract

*Define:* **WBS**

Work Breakdown Structure

*Define:* **VAC**

Variance at Completion

# Definitions

The following definitions are taken directly from the PMBOK Guide (Sixth Edition).

*Define:* **Acceptance Criteria**

A set of conditions that is required to be met before deliverables are accepted.

*Define:* **Accepted Deliverables**

Products, results, or capabilities produced by a project and validated by the project customer or sponsors as meeting their specified acceptance criteria.

*Define:* **Accuracy**

Within the quality management system, accuracy is an assessment of correctness.

*Define:* **Acquire Resources**

The process of obtaining team members, facilities, equipment, materials, supplies, and other resources necessary to complete project work.

*Define:* **Acquisition**

Obtaining human and material resources necessary to perform project activities. Acquisition implies a cost of resources, and is not necessarily financial.

*Define:* **Activity**

A distinct, scheduled portion of work performed during the course of a project.

*Define:* **Activity Attributes**

Multiple attributes associated with each schedule activity that can be included within the activity list. Activity attributes include activity codes, predecessor activities, successor activities, logical relationships, leads and lags, resource requirements, imposed dates, constraints and assumptions.

*Define:* **Activity Duration**

The time in calendar units between the start and finish of a schedule activity. See also duration.

*Define:* **Activity Duration Estimates**

The quantitative assessments of the likely number of time periods that are required to complete an activity.

*Define:* **Activity List**

A documented tabulation of schedule activities that shows the activity description, activity identifier, and a sufficiently detailed scope of work description so project team members understand what work is to be performed.

*Define:* **Activity-on-Node (AON)**

See precedence diagramming method (PDM).

# Definitions

*Define:* **Actual cost (AC)**

The realized cost incurred for the work performed on an activity during a specific time period.

---

*Define:* **Actual Duration**

The time in calendar units between the actual start date of the schedule activity and either the data date of the project schedule if the schedule activity is in progress, or the actual finish date if the schedule activity is complete.

---

*Define:* **Adaptive Life Cycle**

A project life cycle that is iterative or incremental.

---

*Define:* **Affinity Diagrams**

A technique that allows large numbers of ideas to be classified into groups for review and analysis.

---

*Define:* **Agreements**

Any document or communication that defines the initial intentions of a project. This can take the form of a contract, memorandum of understanding (MOU), letters of agreement, verbal agreements, email etc.

---

*Define:* **Alternative Analysis**

A technique used to evaluate identified options in order to select the options or approaches to use to execute and perform the work of the project.

---

*Define:* **Analogous Estimating**

A technique for estimating the duration or cost of an activity or a project using historical data from a similar activity or project.

---

*Define:* **Analytical Techniques**

Various techniques used to evaluate, analyze, or forecast potential outcomes based on possible variations of project or environmental variables and their relationships with other variables.

---

*Define:* **Assumption**

A factor in the planning process that is considered to be true, real, or certain without proof or demonstration.

---

*Define:* **Assumption Log**

A project document used to record all assumptions and constraints throughout the project life cycle.

---

*Define:* **Attribute Sampling**

A method of measuring quality that consists of noting the presence (or absence) of some characteristic (attribute) in each of the units under consideration.

---

*Define:* **Authority**

The right to apply project resources, expend funds, make decisions, or give approvals.

---

# Definitions

*Define:* **Backward Pass**

A critical path method technique for calculating the late start and late finish dates by working backward through the schedule model from the project end date.

*Define:* **Bar Chart**

A graphic display of schedule-related Information. In the typical bar chart, schedule activities or work breakdown structure components are listed down the left side of the chart, dates are shown across the top, and activity durations are shown as date-placed horizontal bars. See also Gantt chart.

*Define:* **Baseline**

The approved version of a work product that can be changed only through formal change control procedures and is used as a basis for comparison to actual results.

*Define:* **Basis of Estimates**

Supporting documentation outlining the details used in establishing project estimates such as assumptions, constraints, level of detail, ranges, and confidence levels.

*Define:* **Benchmarking**

The comparison of actual or planned products, processes, and practices to those of comparable organizations to identify best practices, generate ideas for improvement, and provide a basis for measuring performance.

*Define:* **Benefits Management Plan**

The documented explanation defining the processes for creating, maximizing, and sustaining the benefits provided by a project or program.

*Define:* **Bid Documents**

All documents used to solicit information, quotations, or proposals from prospective sellers.

*Define:* **Bidder Conference**

The meetings with prospective sellers prior to the preparation of a bid or proposal to ensure all prospective vendors have a clear and common understanding of the procurement. Also known as contractor conferences, vendor conferences, or pre-bid conferences.

*Define:* **Bottom-Up Estimating**

A method of estimating project duration or cost by aggregating the estimates of the lower-level components of the work breakdown structure (WBS).

*Define:* **Budget**

The approved estimate for the project or any work breakdown structure component or any schedule activity.

*Define:* **Budget at Completion (BAC)**

The sum of all budgets established for the work to be performed.

*Define:* **Buffer**

See reserve.

*Define:* **Business Case**

A documented economic feasibility study used to establish validity of the benefits of a selected component lacking sufficient definition and that is used as a basis for the authorization of further project management activities.

*Define:* **Business Value**

The net quantifiable benefit derived from a business endeavor. The benefit may be tangible, intangible, or both.

*Define:* **Cause and Effect Diagram**

A decomposition technique that helps trace an undesirable effect back to its root cause.

*Define:* **Change**

A modification to any formally controlled deliverable, project management plan component, or project document.

*Define:* **Change Control**

A process whereby modifications to documents, deliverables, or baselines associated with the project are identified, documented, approved, or rejected.

*Define:* **Change Control Board (CCB)**

A formally chartered group responsible for reviewing, evaluating, approving, delaying, or rejecting changes to the project, and for recording and communicating such decisions.

*Define:* **Change Control System**

A set of procedures that describe how modifications to the project deliverables and documentation are managed and controlled.

*Define:* **Change Control Tools**

Manual or automated tools to assist with change and/or configuration management. At a minimum, the tools should support the activities of the CCB.

*Define:* **Change Log**

A comprehensive list of changes submitted during the project and their current status.

*Define:* **Change Management Plan**

A component of the project management plan that establishes the change control board, documents the extent of its authority, and describes how the change control system will be implemented.

*Define:* **Change Request**

A formal proposal to modify a document, deliverable, or baseline.

*Define:* **Charter**

See project charter.

# Definitions

*Define:* **Checklist Analysis**

A technique for systematically reviewing materials using a list for accuracy and completeness.

---

*Define:* **Check sheet**

A tally sheet that can be used as a checklist when gathering data.

---

*Define:* **Claim**

A request, demand, or assertion of rights by a seller against a buyer, or vice versa, for consideration, compensation, or payment under the terms of a legally binding contract, such as for a disputed change.

---

*Define:* **Context Diagrams**

A visual depiction of the product scope showing a business system (process, equipment, computer system, etc.), and how people and other systems (actors) interact with it.

---

*Define:* **Contingency**

An event or occurrence that could affect the execution of the project that may be accounted for with a reserve.

---

*Define:* **Contingency Reserve**

Time or money allocated in the schedule or cost baseline for known risks with active response strategies.

---

*Define:* **Contingent Response Strategies**

Responses provided which may be used in the event that a specific trigger occurs.

---

*Define:* **Contract**

A mutually binding agreement that obligates the seller to provide the specified product or service or result and obligates the buyer to pay for it.

---

*Define:* **Contract Change Control System**

The system used to collect, track, adjudicate, and communicate changes to a contract.

---

*Define:* **Control**

Comparing actual performance with planned performance, analyzing variances, assessing trends to effect process improvements, evaluating possible alternatives, and recommending appropriate corrective action as needed.

---

*Define:* **Control Account**

A management control point where scope, budget, actual cost, and schedule are integrated and compared to earned value for performance measurement.

---

*Define:* **Control Chart**

A graphic display of process data over time and against established control limits, which has a centerline that assists in detecting a trend of plotted values toward either control limit.

---

# Definitions

*Define:* **Control Costs**

The process of monitoring the status of the project to update the project costs and manage changes to the cost baseline.

*Define:* **Control Limits**

The area composed of three standard deviations on either side of the centerline or mean of a normal distribution of data plotted on a control chart, which reflects the expected variation in the data. See also specification limits.

*Define:* **Control Procurements**

The process of managing procurement relationships, monitoring contract performance, making changes and corrections as appropriate, and closing out contracts.

*Define:* **Control Quality**

The process of monitoring and recording results of executing the quality management activities to assess performance and ensure the project outputs are complete, correct, and meet customer expectations.

*Define:* **Control Resources**

The process of ensuring that the physical resources assigned and allocated to the project are available as planned, as well as monitoring the planned versus actual utilization of resources and performing corrective action as necessary.

*Define:* **Control Schedule**

The process of monitoring the status of the project to update the project schedule and manage changes to the schedule baseline.

*Define:* **Claims Administration**

The process of processing, adjudicating, and communicating contract claims.

*Define:* **Close Project or Phase**

The process of finalizing all activities for the project, phase, or contract.

*Define:* **Closing Process Group**

The process is performed to formally complete or close a project, phase, or contract.

*Define:* **Code of Accounts**

A numbering system used to uniquely identify each component of the work breakdown structure (WBS).

*Define:* **Collect Requirements**

The process of determining, documenting, and managing stakeholder needs and requirements to meet project objectives.

*Define:* **Colocation**

An organizational placement strategy where the project team members are physically located close to one another to improve communication, working relationships, and productivity.

# Definitions

*Define:* **Communication Methods**

A systematic procedure, technique, or process used to transfer information among project stakeholders.

*Define:* **Communication Models**

A description, analogy, or schematic used to represent how the communication process will be performed for the project.

*Define:* **Communication Requirements Analysis**

An analytical technique to determine the information needs of the project stakeholders through interviews, workshops, study of lessons learned from previous projects, etc.

*Define:* **Communications Management Plan**

A component of the project, program, or portfolio management plan that describes how, when, and by whom information about the project will be administered and disseminated.

*Define:* **Communication Styles Assessment**

A technique to identify the preferred communication method, format, and content for stakeholders for planned communication activities.

*Define:* **Communication Technology**

Specific tools, systems, computer programs, etc. used to transfer information among project stakeholders.

*Define:* **Conduct Procurements**

The process of obtaining seller responses, selecting a seller, and awarding a contract.

*Define:* **Configuration Management Plan**

A component of the project management plan that describes how to identify and account for project artifacts under configuration control, and how to record and report changes to them.

*Define:* **Configuration Management System**

A collection of procedures used to track project artifacts and monitor and control changes to these artifacts.

*Define:* **Conformance**

Within the quality management system, conformance is a general concept of delivering results that fall within the limits that define acceptable variation for a quality requirement.

*Define:* **Constraint**

A limiting factor that affects the execution of a project, program, portfolio, or process.

*Define:* **Control Scope**

The process of monitoring the status of the project and product scope and managing changes to the scope baseline

# Definitions

*Define:* **Cost Aggregation**

Summing the lower-level cost estimates with the various work packages for a given level within the project's WBS or for a given cost control account.

---

*Define:* **Cost Baseline**

The approved version of the time-phased project budget excluding any management reserves, which can be changed only through formal change control procedures and is used as a basis for comparison to actual results.

---

*Define:* **Cost-Benefit Analysis**

A financial analysis tool used to determine the benefits provided by a project against its costs.

---

*Define:* **Cost Management Plan**

A component of a project or program management plan that describes how costs will be planned, structured, and controlled.

---

*Define:* **Cost of Quality (COQ)**

All costs incurred over the life of the product by investment in preventing nonconformance to requirements, appraisal of the product or service for conformance to requirements, and failure to meet requirements.

---

*Define:* **Cost Performance Index (CPI)**

A measure of the cost efficiency of budgeted resources expressed as the ratio of earned value to actual cost.

---

*Define:* **Cost Plus Award Fee Contract (CPAF)**

A category of contract that involves payments to the seller for all legitimate actual costs incurred for completed work, plus an award fee representing seller profit.

---

*Define:* **Cost Plus Fixed Fee Contract (CPFF)**

A type of cost-reimbursable contract where the buyer reimburses the seller for the seller's allowable costs (allowable costs are defined by the contract) plus a fixed amount of profit (fee).

---

*Define:* **Cost Plus Incentive Fee Contract (CPIF)**

A type of cost-reimbursable contract where the buyer reimburses the seller for the seller's allowable costs (allowable costs are defined by the contract), and the seller earns its profit if it meets defined performance Criteria.

---

*Define:* **Cost- Reimbursable Contract**

A type of contract involving payment to the seller for the seller's actual costs, plus a fee typically representing the seller's profit.

---

*Define:* **Cost variance**

The amount of budget deficit or surplus at a given point in time, expressed as the difference between the earned value and the actual Cost.

---

*Define:* **Crashing**

A technique used to shorten the schedule duration to the least incremental cost by adding resources.

---

*Define:* **Create WBS**

The process of subdividing project deliverables and project work into smaller, more manageable components.

*Define:* **Criteria**

Standards, rules, or tests on which a judgement or decision can be based or by which a product, service, result, or process can be evaluated.

*Define:* **Critical Path**

The sequence of activities that represents the longest path through a project, which determines the shortest possible duration.

*Define:* **Critical Path Activity**

Any activity on the critical path in a project schedule.

*Define:* **Critical Path Method (CPM)**

A method used to estimate the minimum project duration and determine the amount of schedule flexibility on the logical network paths within the schedule model.

*Define:* **Data**

Discrete, unorganized, unprocessed measurements or raw observations.

*Define:* **Data Analysis Techniques**

Techniques used to organize, assess, and evaluate data and information.

*Define:* **Data Date**

A point in time when the status of the project is recorded

*Define:* **Data Gathering Techniques**

Techniques used to collect data and information from a variety of sources.

*Define:* **Data Representation Techniques**

Graphic representations or other methods used to convey data and information.

*Define:* **Decision-Making Techniques**

Techniques used to select a course of action from different alternatives.

*Define:* **Decision Tree Analysis**

A diagramming and calculation technique for evaluating the implications of a chain of multiple options in the presence of uncertainty.

*Define:* **Decomposition**

A technique used for dividing and subdividing the project scope and project deliverables into smaller, more manageable parts.

# Definitions

*Define:* **Defect**

An imperfection or deficiency in a project component where that component does not meet its requirements or specifications and needs to be either repaired or replaced.

*Define:* **Defect Repair**

An intentional activity to modify a nonconforming product or product component.

*Define:* **Define Activities**

The process of identifying and documenting the specific actions to be performed to produce the project deliverables.

*Define:* **Define Scope**

The process of developing a detailed description of the project and product.

*Define:* **Deliverable**

Any unique and verifiable product result, or capability to perform a service that is required to be produced to complete a process, phase, or project.

*Define:* **Dependency**

See logical relationship

*Define:* **Determine Budget**

The process of aggregating the estimated costs of individual activities or work packages to establish an authorized cost baseline.

*Define:* **Development Approach**

The method used to create and evolve the product, service, or result during the project life cycle, such as predictive, iterative, incremental, agile, or a hybrid method.

*Define:* **Develop Project Charter**

The process of developing a document that formally authorizes the existence of a project and provides the project manager with the authority to apply organizational resources to project activities.

*Define:* **Develop Project Management Plan**

The process of defining, preparing, and coordinating all plan components and consolidating them into an integrated project management plan.

*Define:* **Develop Schedule**

The process of analyzing activity sequences, durations, resource requirements, and schedule constraints to create the project schedule model for project execution and monitoring and controlling.

*Define:* **Develop Team**

The process of improving competences, team member interaction, and overall team environment to enhance project performance.

# Definitions

*Define:* **Diagramming Techniques**

Approaches to presenting information with logical linkages that aid in understanding.

---

*Define:* **Direct and Manage Project Work**

The process of leading and performing the work defined in the project management plan and implementing approved changes to achieve the project's objectives.

---

*Define:* **Discrete Effort**

An activity that can be planned and measured and that yields a specific output. [Note: Discrete effort is one of three earned value management (EVM) types of activities used to measure work performance.]

---

*Define:* **Discretionary Dependency**

A relationship that is established based on knowledge of best practices within a particular application area or an aspect of the project where a specific sequence is desired.

---

*Define:* **Documentation Reviews**

The process of gathering a corpus of information and reviewing it to determine accuracy and completeness.

---

*Define:* **Duration**

The total number of work periods required to complete an activity or work breakdown structure component, expressed in hours, days, or weeks. Contrast with effort.

---

*Define:* **Early Finish Date (EF)**

In the critical path method, the earliest possible point in time when the uncompleted portions of a schedule activity can finish based on the schedule network logic, the data date, and any schedule constraints.

---

*Define:* **Early Start Date (ES)**

In the critical path method, the earliest possible point in time when the uncompleted portions of a schedule activity can start based on the schedule network logic, the data date, and any schedule constraints.

---

*Define:* **Earned Value (EV)**

The measure of work performed expressed in terms of the budget authorized for that work.

---

*Define:* **Earned Value Management**

A methodology that combines scope, schedule, and resource measurements to assess project performance and progress.

---

*Define:* **Effort**

The number of labor units required to complete a schedule activity or work breakdown structure component, often expressed in hours, days, or weeks. Contrast with duration.

---

*Define:* **Emotional intelligence**

The ability to identify, assess, and manage the personal emotions of oneself and other people, as well as the collective emotions of groups of people.

---

*Define:* **EEFs**

Conditions, not under the immediate control of the team, that influence, constrain, or direct the project, program, or portfolio.

*Define:* **Estimate**

A quantitative assessment of the likely amount or outcome of a variable, such as project costs, resources, effort, or durations.

*Define:* **Estimate Activity Durations**

The process of estimating the number of work periods needed to complete individual activities with the estimated resources.

*Define:* **Estimate Activity Resources**

The process of estimating team resources and the type and quantities of material, equipment and supplies necessary to perform project work.

*Define:* **Estimate at Completion (EAC)**

The expected total cost of completing all work expressed as the sum of the actual cost to date and the estimate to complete.

*Define:* **Estimate Costs**

The process of developing an approximation of the monetary resources needed to complete project work.

*Define:* **Estimate to Complete (ETC)**

The expected cost to finish all the remaining project work.

*Define:* **Execute**

Directing, managing performing and accomplishing the project work; providing the deliverables; and providing work performance information.

*Define:* **Executing Process Group**

Those processes performed to complete the work defined in the project management plan to satisfy the project requirements.

*Define:* **Expert Judgment**

Judgment provided based upon expertise in an application area, knowledge area, discipline, industry, etc. as appropriate for the activity being performed. Such expertise may be provided by any group or person with specialized education, knowledge skill, experience or training.

*Define:* **Explicit Knowledge**

Knowledge that can be codified using symbols such as words, numbers, and pictures.

*Define:* **External Dependency**

A relationship between project activities and non-project activities.

# Definitions

*Define:* **Fallback Plan**

Fallback plans include an alternative set of actions and tasks available in the event that the primary plan needs to be abandoned because of issues, risks, or other causes.

*Define:* **Fast Tracking**

A schedule compression technique in which activities or phases normally done in sequence are performed in parallel for at least a portion of their duration.

*Define:* **Fee**

Represents profit as a component of compensation to a seller.

*Define:* **Finish Date**

A point in time associated with a schedule activity's completion. Usually qualified by one of the following: actual, planned, estimated, scheduled, early, late, baseline, target, or current.

*Define:* **Finish-to-Finish (FF)**

A logical relationship in which a successor activity cannot finish until a predecessor activity has finished.

*Define:* **Finish-to-Start (FS)**

A logical relationship in which a successor activity cannot start until a predecessor activity has finished.

*Define:* **Firm Fixed Price Contract (FFP)**

A type of fixed price contract where the buyer pays the seller a set amount (as defined by the contract), regardless of the seller's costs.

*Define:* **Fishbone diagram**

See Cause and Effect Diagram.

*Define:* **Fixed-Price Contract**

An agreement that sets the fee that will be paid for a defined scope of work regardless of the cost or effort to deliver it.

*Define:* **Fixed Price Incentive Fee Contract (FPIF)**

A type of contract where the buyer pays the seller a set amount (as defined by the contract), and the seller can earn an additional amount if the seller meets defined performance criteria.

*Define:* **Fixed Price with Economic Price Adjustment Contract (FPEPA)**

A fixed-price contract, but with a special provision allowing for predefined final adjustments to the contract price due to changed conditions, such as inflation changes, or cost increases (or decreases) for specific commodities.

*Define:* **Float**

Also called slack. See total float and free float.

# Definitions

*Define:* **Flowchart**

The depletion in a diagram format of the inputs, process actions, and outputs of one or more processes within a system.

*Define:* **Focus Groups**

An elicitation technique that brings together prequalified stakeholders and subject matter experts to learn about their expectations and attitudes about a proposed product, service, or result.

*Define:* **Forecast**

An estimate or prediction of conditions and events in the project's future based on information and knowledge available at the time of the forecast.

*Define:* **Forward Pass**

A critical path method technique for calculating the early start and early finish dates by working ton/yard through the schedule model from the project start date or a given point in time.

*Define:* **Free Float**

The amount of time that a schedule activity can be delayed without delaying the early start date of any successor or violating a schedule constraint.

*Define:* **Functional Organization**

An organizational structure in which staff is grouped by areas of specialization and the project manager has limited authority to assign work and apply resources.

*Define:* **Funding Limit Reconciliation**

The process of comparing the planned expenditure of project funds against any limits on the commitment of funds for the project to identify any variances between the funding limits and the planned expenditures.

*Define:* **Gantt Chart**

A bar chart of schedule information where activities are listed on the vertical axis, dates are shown on the horizontal axis, and activity durations are shown as horizontal bars placed according to start and finish dates.

*Define:* **Grade**

A category or rank used to distinguish items that have the same functional use but do not share the same requirements for quality.

*Define:* **Ground Rules**

Expectations regarding acceptable behavior by project team members.

*Define:* **Histogram**

A bar chart that shows the graphical representation of numerical data.

*Define:* **Historical Information**

Documents and data on prior projects including project files, records, correspondence, closed contracts, and closed projects.

# Definitions

*Define:* **Identify Risks**

The process of identifying individual risks as well as sources of overall risk and documenting their characteristics.

*Define:* **Identify Stakeholders**

The process of identifying project stakeholders regularly and analyzing and documenting relevant information regarding their interests, involvement, interdependencies, influence, and potential impact on project success.

*Define:* **Implement Risk Responses**

The process of implementing agreed-upon risk response plans.

*Define:* **Imposed Date**

A fixed date imposed on a schedule activity or schedule milestone, usually in the form of a "start no earlier than" and "finish no later than" date.

*Define:* **Incentive Fee**

A set of financial incentives related to cost, schedule, or technical performance of the seller.

*Define:* **Incremental Life Cycle**

An adaptive project life cycle in which the deliverable is produced through a series of iterations that successively add functionality within a predetermined time frame. The deliverable contains the necessary and sufficient capability to be considered complete only after the final iteration.

*Define:* **Independent Estimates**

A process of using a third party to obtain and analyze information to support prediction of cost, schedule, or other items.

*Define:* **Influence Diagram**

A graphical representation of situations showing causal influences, time ordering of events, and other relationships among variables and outcomes.

*Define:* **Information**

Organized or structured data, processed for a specific purpose to make it meaningful, valuable, and useful in specific contexts.

*Define:* **Information Management Systems**

Facilities, processes, and procedures used to collect, store, and distribute information between producers and consumers of information in physical or electronic format.

*Define:* **Initiating Process Group**

Those processes performed to define a new project or a new phase of an existing project by obtaining authorization to start the project or phase.

*Define:* **Input**

Any item, whether internal or external to the project, which is required by a process before that process proceeds. May be an output from a predecessor process.

# Definitions

*Define:* **Inspection**

Examination of a work product to determine whether it conforms to documented standards.

*Define:* **Interpersonal and Team Skills**

Skills used to effectively lead and interact with team members and other stakeholders.

*Define:* **Interpersonal Skills**

Skills used to establish and maintain relationships with other people.

*Define:* **Interviews**

A formal or informal approach to elicit information from stakeholders by talking to them directly.

*Define:* **Invitation for Bid (IFB)**

Generally, this term is equivalent to request for proposal However, in some application areas, it may have a narrower or more specific meaning.

*Define:* **Issue**

A current condition or situation that may have an impact on the project objectives.

*Define:* **Issue Log**

A project document where information about issues is recorded and monitored.

*Define:* **Iterative Life Cycle**

A project life cycle where the project scope is generally determined early in the project life cycle, but time and cost estimates are routinely modified as the project team's understanding of the product increases. Iterations develop the product through a series of repeated cycles, while increments successively add to the functionality of the product.

*Define:* **Knowledge**

A mixture of experience, values and beliefs, contextual information, intuition and insight that people use to make sense of new experiences and information.

*Define:* **Lag**

The amount of time whereby a successor activity will be delayed with respect to a predecessor activity.

*Define:* **Late Finish Date (LF)**

In the critical path method, the latest possible point in time when the uncompleted portions of a schedule activity can finish based on the schedule network logic, the project completion date, and any schedule constraints.

*Define:* **Late Start Date (LS)**

In the critical path method, the latest possible point in time when the uncompleted portions of a schedule activity can start based on the schedule network logic, the project completion date, and any schedule constraints.

# Definitions

*Define:* **Lead**

The amount of time whereby a successor activity can be advanced with respect to a predecessor activity.

*Define:* **Lessons Learned**

The knowledge gained during a project which shows how project events were addressed or should be addressed in the future for the purpose of improving future performance.

*Define:* **Lessons Learned Register**

A project document used to record knowledge gained during a project so that it can be used in the current project and entered into the lessons learned repository.

*Define:* **Lessons Learned Repository**

A store of historical Information about lessons learned in projects.

*Define:* **Level of Effort (LOE)**

An activity that does not produce definitive end products and is measured by the passage of time.

*Define:* **Life Cycle**

See project life cycle.

*Define:* **Log**

A document used to record and describe or denote selected items identified during execution of a process or activity. Usually used with a modifier, such as issue, change, issue, or assumption.

*Define:* **Logical Relationship**

A dependency between two activities, or between an activity and a milestone.

*Define:* **Make-or-Buy Analysis**

The process of gathering and organizing data about product requirements and analyzing them against available alternatives including the purchase or internal manufacture of the product.

*Define:* **Make-or-Buy Decisions**

Decisions made regarding the external purchase or internal manufacture of a product.

*Define:* **Manage Communications**

Manage Communications is the process of ensuring timely and appropriate collection, creation, distribution, storage, retrieval, management, monitoring, and the ultimate disposition of project information.

*Define:* **Management Reserve**

An amount of the project budget or project schedule held outside of the performance measurement baseline (PMB) for management control purposes, that is reserved for unforeseen work that is within scope of the project.

# Definitions

*Define:* **Management Skills**

The ability to plan, organize, direct, and control individuals or groups of people to achieve specific goals.

---

*Define:* **Manage Project Knowledge**

The process of using existing knowledge and creating new knowledge to achieve the project's objectives and contribute to organizational learning.

---

*Define:* **Manage Quality**

The process of translating the quality management plan into executable quality activities that incorporate the organization's quality policies into the project.

---

*Define:* **Manage Stakeholder Engagement**

The process of communicating and working with stakeholders to meet their needs and expectations, address issues, and foster appropriate stakeholder involvement.

---

*Define:* **Manage Team**

The process of tracking team member performance, providing feedback, resolving issues, and managing team changes to optimize project performance.

---

*Define:* **Mandatory Dependency**

A relationship that is contractually required or inherent in the nature of the work.

---

*Define:* **Master Schedule**

A summary-level project schedule that identifies the major deliverables and work breakdown structure components and key schedule milestones. See also milestone schedule.

---

*Define:* **Matrix Diagrams**

A quality management and control tool used to perform data analysis within the organizational structure created in the matrix. The matrix diagram seeks to show the strength of relationships between factors, causes, and objectives that exist between the rows and columns that form the matrix.

---

*Define:* **Matrix Organization**

Any organizational structure in which the project manager shares responsibility with the functional managers for assigning priorities and for directing the work of persons assigned to the project.

---

*Define:* **Methodology**

A system of practices, techniques, procedures, and rules used by those who work in a discipline.

---

*Define:* **Milestone**

A significant point or event in a project, program, or portfolio.

---

*Define:* **Milestone Schedule**

A type of schedule that presents milestones with planned dates. See also master schedule.

---

# Definitions

*Define:* **Mind-Mapping**

A technique used to consolidate ideas created through individual brainstorming sessions into a single map to reflect commonality and differences in understanding and to generate new ideas.

*Define:* **Monitor**

Collect project performance data, produce performance measures, and report and disseminate performance information.

*Define:* **Monitor and Control Project Work**

The process of tracking, reviewing, and reporting overall progress to meet the performance objectives defined in the project management plan.

*Define:* **Monitor Communications**

The process of ensuring that the information needs of the project and its stakeholders are met.

*Define:* **Monitoring and Controlling Process Group**

Those processes required to track, review, and regulate the progress and performance of the project; identify any areas in which changes to the plan are required; and initiate the corresponding changes.

*Define:* **Monitor Risks**

The process of monitoring the implementation of agreed-upon risk response plans, tracking identified risks, identifying and analyzing new risks, and evaluating risk process effectiveness throughout the project.

*Define:* **Monitor Stakeholder Engagement**

The process of monitoring project stakeholder relationships, and tailoring strategies for engaging stakeholders through the modification of engagement strategies and plans.

*Define:* **Monte Carlo Simulation**

An analysis technique where a computer model is iterated many times, with the input values chosen at random for each iteration driven by the input data, including probability distributions and probabilistic branches. Outputs are generated to represent the range of possible outcomes for the project.

*Define:* **Multicriteria Decision Analysis**

This technique utilizes a decision matrix to provide a systematic analytical approach for establishing criteria, such as risk levels, uncertainty, and valuation, to evaluate and rank many ideas.

*Define:* **Network**

See project schedule network diagram.

*Define:* **Network Logic**

All activity dependencies in a project schedule network diagram.

*Define:* **Network Path**

A sequence of activities connected by logical relationships in a project schedule network diagram.

# Definitions

*Define:* **Networking**

Establishing connections and relationships with other people from the same or other organizations.

---

*Define:* **Node**

A point at which dependency lines connect on a schedule network diagram.

---

*Define:* **Nominal Group Technique**

A technique that enhances brainstorming with a voting process used to rank the most useful ideas for further brainstorming or for prioritization.

---

*Define:* **Objective**

Something toward which work is to be directed, a strategic position to be attained, a purpose to be achieved, a result to be obtained, a product to be produced, or a service to be performed.

---

*Define:* **Opportunity**

A risk that would have a positive effect on one or more project objectives.

---

*Define:* **Organizational Breakdown Structure (OBS)**

A hierarchical representation of the project organization, which illustrates the relationship between project activities and the organizational units that will perform those activities.

---

*Define:* **Organizational Learning**

A discipline concerned with the way individuals, groups, and organizations develop knowledge.

---

*Define:* **Organizational Process Assets**

Plans, processes, policies, procedures, and knowledge bases that are specific to and used by the performing organization

---

*Define:* **Output**

A product, result or service generated by a process. May be an input to a successor process.

---

*Define:* **Overall Project Risk**

The effect of uncertainty on the project as a whole, arising from all sources of uncertainty including individual risks, representing the exposure of stakeholders to the implications of variations in project outcome both positive and negative.

---

*Define:* **Parametric Estimating**

An estimating technique in which an algorithm is used to calculate cost or duration based on historical data and project parameters.

---

*Define:* **Path Convergence**

A relationship in which a schedule activity has more than one predecessor.

---

*Define:* **Path Divergence**

A relationship in which a schedule activity has more than one successor.

---

# Definitions

*Define:* **Percent Complete**

An estimate expressed as a percent of the amount of work that has been completed on an activity or a work breakdown structure component.

*Define:* **Performance Measurement Baseline (PMB)**

Integrated scope schedule, and cost baselines used for comparison to manage, measure, and control project execution.

*Define:* **Performance Reviews**

A technique that is used to measure, compare, and analyze actual performance of work in progress on the project against the baseline.

*Define:* **Perform integrated Change Control**

The process of reviewing all change requests, approving changes and managing changes to deliverables, organizational process assets, project documents, and the project management plan; and communicating the decisions.

*Define:* **Perform Qualitative Risk Analysis**

The process of prioritizing individual project risks for further analyses or action by assessing their probability of occurrence and impact as well as other characteristics.

*Define:* **Perform Quantitative Risk Analysis**

The process of numerically analyzing the combined effect of identified individual project risks and other sources of uncertainty on overall project objectives.

*Define:* **Phase**

See project phase.

*Define:* **Phase Gate**

A review at the end of a phase in which a decision is made to continue to the next phase, to continue with modification, or to end a project or program.

*Define:* **Plan Communications Management**

The process of developing an appropriate approach and plan for project communication activities based on the information needs of each stakeholder or group, available organizational assets, and the needs of the project.

*Define:* **Plan Cost Management**

The process of defining how the project costs will be estimated, budgeted managed, monitored and controlled.

*Define:* **Planned Value (PV)**

The authorized budget assigned to scheduled work.

*Define:* **Planning Package**

A work breakdown structure component below the control account with known work content but without detailed schedule activities. See also control account.

# Definitions

*Define:* **Planning Process Group**

Those processes required to establish the scope of the project, refine the objectives, and define the course of action required to attain the objectives that the project was undertaken to achieve.

---

*Define:* **Plan Procurement Management**

The process of documenting project procurement decisions, specifying the approach, and identifying potential sellers.

---

*Define:* **Plan Quality Management**

The process of identifying quality requirements and/or standards for the project and its deliverables and documenting how the project will demonstrate compliance with quality requirements and/or standards.

---

*Define:* **Plan Resource Management**

The process of defining how to estimate, acquire, manage, and utilize physical and team resources.

---

*Define:* **Plan Risk Management**

The process of defining how to conduct risk management activities for a project.

---

*Define:* **Plan Risk Responses**

The process of developing options, selecting strategies, and agreeing on actions to address overall project risk exposure as well as to treat individual project risks.

---

*Define:* **Plan Schedule Management**

The process of establishing the policies, procedures, and documentation for planning, developing, managing, executing, and controlling the project schedule.

---

*Define:* **Plan Scope Management**

The process of creating a scope management plan that documents how the project and product scope will be defined, validated, and controlled.

---

*Define:* **Plan Stakeholder Engagement**

The process of developing approaches to involve project stakeholders based on their needs, expectations, interests, and potential impact on the project.

---

*Define:* **Plurality**

Decisions made by the largest block in a group, even if a majority is not achieved.

---

*Define:* **Policy**

A structured pattern of actions adopted by an organization such that the organization's policy can be explained as a set of basic principles that govern the organization's conduct.

---

*Define:* **Portfolio**

Projects, programs, subsidiary portfolios, and operations managed as a group to achieve strategic objectives.

---

*Define:* **Portfolio Management**

The centralized management of one or more portfolios to achieve strategic objectives.

*Define:* **Practice**

A specific type of professional or management activity that contributes to the execution of a process and that may employ one or more techniques and tools.

*Define:* **Precedence Diagramming Method (PDM)**

A technique used for constructing a schedule model in which activities are represented by nodes and are graphically linked by one or more logical relationships to show the sequence in which the activities are to be performed.

*Define:* **Precedence Relationship**

A logical dependency used in the precedence diagramming method.

*Define:* **Predecessor Activity**

An activity that logically comes before a dependent activity in a schedule.

*Define:* **Predictive Life Cycle**

A form of project life cycle in which the project scope, time, and cost are determined in the early phases of the life cycle.

*Define:* **Preventive Action**

An intentional activity that ensures the future performance of the project work is aligned with the project management plan.

*Define:* **Probability and Impact Matrix**

A grid for mapping the probability of occurrence of each risk and its impact on project objectives if that risk occurs.

*Define:* **Procedure**

An established method of accomplishing a consistent performance or result, a procedure typically can be described as the sequence of steps that will be used to execute a process.

*Define:* **Process**

A systematic series of activities directed towards causing an end result such that one or more inputs will be acted upon to create one or more outputs.

*Define:* **Procurement Audits**

The review of contracts and contracting processes for completeness, accuracy, and effectiveness.

*Define:* **Procurement Documents**

The documents utilized in bid and proposal activities, which include the buyer's invitation for bid, invitation for negotiations, request for information, request for quotation, request for proposal, and seller's responses.

# Definitions

*Define:* **Procurement Documentation**

All documents used in signing, executing, and closing an agreement. Procurement documentation may include documents predating the project.

*Define:* **Procurement Management Plan**

A component of the project or program management plan that describes how a project team will acquire goods and services from outside of the performing organization.

*Define:* **Procurement Statement of Work**

Describes the procurement item in sufficient detail to allow prospective sellers to determine if they are capable of providing the products, services, or results.

*Define:* **Procurement Strategy**

The approach by the buyer to determine the project delivery method and the type of legally binding agreement(s) that should be used to deliver the desired results

*Define:* **Product**

An artifact that is produced, is quantifiable, and can be either an end item in itself or a component item. Additional words for products are material and goods. See also deliverable.

*Define:* **Product Analysis**

For projects that have a product as a deliverable, it is a tool to define scope that generally means asking questions about a product and forming answers to describe the use, characteristics, and other relevant aspects of what is going to be manufactured.

*Define:* **Product Life Cycle**

The series of phases that represent the evolution of a product, from concept through delivery, growth, maturity and to retirement.

*Define:* **Product Scope**

The features and functions that characterize a product, service, or result.

*Define:* **Product Scope Description**

The documented narrative description of the product scope.

*Define:* **Program**

Related projects, subsidiary programs, and program activities that are managed in a coordinated manner to obtain benefits not available from managing them individually.

*Define:* **Program Management**

The application of knowledge, skills, and principles to a program to achieve the program objectives and obtain benefits and control not available by managing program components individually.

*Define:* **Progressive Elaboration**

The iterative process of increasing the level of detail in a project management plan as greater amounts of information and more accurate estimates become available.

# Definitions

*Define:* **Project**

A temporary endeavor undertaken to create a unique product, service, or result.

*Define:* **Project Calendar**

A calendar that Identifies working days and shifts that are available for scheduled activities.

*Define:* **Project Charter**

A document issued by the project initiator or sponsor that formally authorizes the existence of a project and provides the project manager with the authority to apply organizational resources to project activities.

*Define:* **Project Communications Management**

Project Communications Management includes the processes required to ensure timely and appropriate planning, collection, creation, distribution, storage, retrieval, management, control monitoring, and ultimate disposition of project information.

*Define:* **Project Cost Management**

Project Cost Management includes the processes involved in planning, estimating, budgeting, financing, funding, managing, and controlling costs so the project can be completed within the approved budget.

*Define:* **Project Funding Requirements**

Forecast project costs to be paid that are derived from the cost baseline for total or periodic requirements, including projected expenditures plus anticipated liabilities.

*Define:* **Project Governance**

The framework, functions, and processes that guide project management activities in order to create a unique product, service, or result to meet organizational, strategic, and operational goals.

*Define:* **Project Initiation**

Launching a process that can result in the authorization of a new project.

*Define:* **Project Integration Management**

Project integration Management includes the processes and activities to identify, define, combine, unify, and coordinate the various processes and project management activities within the Project Management Process Groups.

*Define:* **Project Life Cycle**

The series of phases that a project passes through from its start to its completion.

*Define:* **Project Management**

The application of knowledge, skills, tools, and techniques to project activities to meet the project requirements.

*Define:* **Project Management Body of Knowledge**

A term that describes the knowledge within the profession of project management. The project management body of knowledge includes proven traditional practices that are widely applied as well as innovative practices that are emerging in the profession

### Define: Project Management Information System

An information system consisting of the tools and techniques used to gather, integrate, and disseminate the outputs of project management processes.

### Define: Project Management Knowledge Area

An identified-area project management defined by its knowledge requirements and described in terms of its component processes practices, inputs, outputs, tools, and techniques.

### Define: Project Management Office (PMB)

A management structure that standardizes the project-related governance processes and facilitates the sharing of resources, methodologies, tools, and techniques.

### Define: Project Management Plan

The document that describes how the project will be executed, monitored and controlled, and closed.

### Define: Project Management Process Group

A logical grouping of project management inputs, tools and techniques, and outputs. The Project Management Process Groups include initiating processes, planning processes, executing processes, monitoring and controlling processes, and closing processes. Project Management Process Groups are not project phases.

### Define: Project Management System

The aggregation of the processes, tools, techniques, methodologies, resources, and procedures to manage a project.

### Define: Project Management Team

The members of the project team who are directly involved in project management activities. See also Project Team.

### Define: Project Manager (PM)

The person assigned by the performing organization to lead the team that is responsible for achieving the project objectives.

### Define: Project Organization Chart

A document that graphically depicts the project team members and their interrelationships for a specific project.

### Define: Project Phase

A collection of logically related project activities that culminates in the completion of one or more deliverables.

### Define: Project Procurement Management

Project Procurement Management includes the processes necessary to purchase or acquire products, services, or results needed from outside the project team.

### Define: Project Quality Management

Project Quality Management includes the processes for incorporating the organization's quality policy regarding planning, managing, and controlling project and product quality requirements, in order to meet stakeholders' expectations.

# Definitions

*Define:* **Project Resource Management**

Project Resource Management includes the processes to identify, acquire, and manage the resources needed for the successful completion of the project.

*Define:* **Project Risk Management**

Project Risk Management includes the processes of conducting risk management planning, identification, analysis, response planning, response implementation, and monitoring risk on a project.

*Define:* **Project Schedule**

An output of a schedule model that presents linked activities with planned dates, durations, milestones, and resources.

*Define:* **Project Schedule Management**

Project Schedule Management includes the processes required to manage the timely completion of the project.

*Define:* **Project Schedule Network Diagram**

A graphical representation of the logical relationships among the project schedule activities.

*Define:* **Project Scope**

The work performed to deliver a product, service, or result with the specified features and functions.

*Define:* **Project Scope Management**

Project Scope Management includes the processes required to ensure that the project includes all the work required, and only the work required, to complete the project successfully.

*Define:* **Project Scope Statement**

The description of the project scope, major deliverables, assumptions, and constraints.

*Define:* **Project Stakeholder Management**

Project Stakeholder Management includes the processes required to identify the people, groups, or organizations that could impact or be impacted by the project, to analyze stakeholder expectations and their impact on the project, and to develop appropriate management strategies for effectively engaging stakeholders in project decisions and execution.

*Define:* **Project Team**

A set of individuals who support the project manager in performing the work of the project to achieve its objectives. See also Project Management Team.

*Define:* **Project Team Directory**

A documented list of project team members, their project roles, and communication information.

*Define:* **Proposal Evaluation Techniques**

The process of reviewing proposals provided by suppliers to support contract award decisions.

*Define:* **Prototypes**

A method of obtaining early feedback on requirements by providing a working model of the expected product before actually building it.

*Define:* **Quality**

The degree to which a set of inherent characteristics fulfills requirements.

*Define:* **Quality Audits**

A quality audit is a structured, independent process to determine if project activities comply with organizational and project policies, processes and procedures.

*Define:* **Quality Checklists**

A structured tool used to verify that a set of required steps has been performed.

*Define:* **Quality Control Measurements**

The documented results of control quality activities.

*Define:* **Quality Management Plan**

A component of the project or program management plan that describes how applicable policies, procedures, and guidelines will be implemented to achieve the quality objectives.

*Define:* **Quality Management System**

The organizational framework whose structure provides the policies, processes, procedures, and resources required to implement the quality management plan. The typical project quality management plan should compatible with the organization's quality management system.

*Define:* **Quality Metrics**

A description of a project or product attribute and how to measure it.

*Define:* **Quality Policy**

A policy specific to the Project Quality Management Knowledge Area, it establishes the basic principles that should govern the organization's actions as it implements its system for quality management.

*Define:* **Quality Report**

A project document that includes quality management issues, recommendations for corrective actions, and a summary of findings from quality control activities and may include recommendations for process, project, and product improvements.

*Define:* **Quality Requirement**

A condition or capability that will be used to assess conformance by validating the acceptability of an attribute for the quality of a result.

*Define:* **Questionnaires**

Written sets of questions designed to quickly accumulate information from a large number of respondents.

# Definitions

*Define:* **RACI Chart**

A common type of responsibility assignment matrix that uses responsible, accountable, consult, and inform statuses to define the involvement of stakeholders in project activities.

---

*Define:* **Regression Analysis**

An analytical technique where a series of input variables are examined in relation to their corresponding output results in order to develop a mathematical or statistical relationship.

---

*Define:* **Regulations**

Requirements imposed by a governmental body. These requirements can establish product, process, or service characteristics, including applicable administrative provisions that have government-mandated compliance.

---

*Define:* **Request for Information (RFI)**

A type of procurement document whereby the buyer requests a potential seller to provide various pieces of information related to a product or service or seller capability.

---

*Define:* **Request for Proposal (RFP)**

A type of procurement document used to request proposals from prospective sellers of products or services. In some application areas, it may have a narrower or more specific meaning.

---

*Define:* **Request for Quotation (RFC)**

A type of procurement document used to request price quotations from prospective sellers of common or standard products or services. Sometimes used in place of request for proposal and, in some application areas, it may have a narrower or more specific meaning.

---

*Define:* **Requirement**

A condition or capability that is necessary to be present in a product, service, or result to satisfy a business need.

---

*Define:* **Requirements Documentation**

A description of how individual requirements meet the business need for the project.

---

*Define:* **Requirements Management Plan**

A component of the project or program management plan that describes how requirements will be analyzed, documented, and managed.

---

*Define:* **Requirements Traceability Matrix**

A grid that links product requirements from their origin to the deliverables that satisfy them.

---

*Define:* **Reserve**

A provision in the project management plan to mitigate cost and/or schedule risk. Often used with a modifier (e.g. management reserve, contingency reserve) to provide further detail on what types of risk are meant to be mitigated.

# Definitions

*Define:* **Reserve Analysis**

An analytical technique to determine the essential features and relationships of components in the project management plan to establish a reserve for the schedule duration, budget, estimated cost, or funds for a project.

*Define:* **Residual Risk**

The risk that remains after risk responses have been implemented.

*Define:* **Resource**

A team member or any physical Item needed to complete the project.

*Define:* **Resource Breakdown Structure (RBS)**

A hierarchical representation of resources by category and type.

*Define:* **Resource Calendar**

A calendar that identifies the working days and shifts upon which each specific resource is available.

*Define:* **Resource Leveling**

A resource optimization technique in which adjustments are made to the project schedule to optimize the allocation of resources and which may affect critical path. See also resource optimization technique and resource smoothing.

*Define:* **Resource Management Plan**

A component of the project management plan that describes how new project resources are acquired, allocated, monitored and controlled.

*Define:* **Resource Manager**

An individual with management authority over one or more resources.

*Define:* **Resource Optimization Technique**

A technique in which activity start and finish dates are adjusted to balance demand for resources with the available supply. See also resource leveling and resource smoothing.

*Define:* **Resource Requirements**

The types and quantities of resources required for each activity in a work package.

*Define:* **Resource Smoothing**

A resource optimization technique in which free and total float are used without affecting the critical path. See also resource leveling and resource optimization technique.

*Define:* **Responsibility**

An assignment that can be delegated within a project management plan such that the assigned resource incurs a duty to perform the requirements of the assignment.

# Definitions

*Define:* **Responsibility Assignment Matrix (RAM)**

A grid that shows the project resources assigned to each work package.

---

*Define:* **Result**

An output from performing project management processes and activities. Results include outcomes (e. g. integrated systems, revised process, restructured organization, tests, trained personnel, etc.) and documents (e. g., policies, plans, studies, procedures, specifications, reports, etc.). See also deliverable.

---

*Define:* **Rework**

Action taken to bring a defective or nonconforming component into Compliance with requirements or specifications.

---

*Define:* **Risk**

An uncertain event or condition that, if it occurs, has a positive or negative effect on one or more project objectives.

---

*Define:* **Risk Acceptance**

A risk response strategy whereby the project team decides to acknowledge the risk and not take any action unless the risk occurs.

---

*Define:* **Risk Appetite**

The degree of uncertainty an organization or individual is willing to accept in anticipation of a reward.

---

*Define:* **Risk Audit**

A type of audit used to consider the effectiveness of the risk management process.

---

*Define:* **Risk Avoidance**

A risk response strategy whereby the project team acts to eliminate the threat or protect the project from its impact.

---

*Define:* **Risk Breakdown Structure (RBS)**

A hierarchical representation of potential sources of risks.

---

*Define:* **Risk Categorization**

Organization by sources of risk (e.gg. using the RBS), the area of the project affected (e.g., using the WBS), or other useful category (e.g., project phase) to determine the areas of the project most exposed to the effects of uncertainty.

---

*Define:* **Risk Category**

A group of potential causes of risk.

---

*Define:* **Risk Data Quality Assessment**

A technique to evaluate the degree to which the data about risks is useful for risk management.

---

*Define:* **Risk Enhancement**

A risk response strategy whereby the project team acts to increase the probability of occurrence or impact of an opportunity.

---

# Definitions

*Define:* **Risk Escalation**

A risk response strategy whereby the team acknowledges that a risk is outside of its sphere of influence and shifts the ownership of the risk to a higher level of the organization where it is more effectively managed.

*Define:* **Risk Exploiting**

A risk response strategy whereby the project team acts to ensure that an opportunity occurs.

*Define:* **Risk Exposure**

An aggregate measure of the potential impact of all risks at any given point in time in a project, program or portfolio.

*Define:* **Risk Management Plan**

A component of the project program, or portfolio management plan that describes how risk management activities will be structured and performed.

*Define:* **Risk Mitigation**

A risk response strategy whereby the project team acts to decrease the probability of occurrence or impact of a threat.

*Define:* **Risk Owner**

The person responsible for monitoring the risks and for selecting and implementing an appropriate risk response strategy.

*Define:* **Risk Register**

A repository in which outputs of risk management processes are recorded.

*Define:* **Risk Report**

A project document developed progressively throughout the Project Risk Management processes, which summarizes information on individual project risks and the level of overall project risk.

*Define:* **Risk Review**

A meeting to examine and document the effectiveness of risk responses in dealing with overall project risk and with identified individual project risks.

*Define:* **Risk Sharing**

A risk response strategy whereby the project team allocates ownership of an opportunity to a third party who is best able to capture the benefit of that opportunity.

*Define:* **Risk Threshold**

The level of risk exposure above which risks are addressed and below which risks may be accepted.

*Define:* **Risk Transference**

A risk response strategy whereby the project team shifts the impact of a threat to a third party, together with ownership of the response.

# Definitions

*Define:* **Role**

A defined function to be performed by a project team member, such as testing, filing, inspecting, or coding.

---

*Define:* **Rolling Wave Planning**

An iterative planning technique in which the work to be accomplished in the near term is planned in detail, while the work in the future is planned at a higher level.

---

*Define:* **Root Cause Analysis**

An analytical technique used to determine the basic underlying reason that causes a variance, defect or a risk. A root cause may underlie more than one variance, defect, risk.

---

*Define:* **Schedule**

See project schedule and schedule model.

---

*Define:* **Schedule Baseline**

The approved version of a schedule model that can be changed using formal change control procedures and is used as the basis for comparison to actual results.

---

*Define:* **Schedule Compression**

A technique used to shorten the schedule duration without reducing the project scope.

---

*Define:* **Schedule Data**

The collection of information for describing and controlling the schedule.

---

*Define:* **Schedule Forecasts**

Estimates or predictions of conditions and events in the project's future based on information and knowledge available at the time the schedule is calculated.

---

*Define:* **Schedule Management Plan**

A component of the project or program management plan that establishes the criteria and the activities for developing, monitoring, and controlling the schedule.

---

*Define:* **Schedule Model**

A representation of the plan for executing the project's activities including durations, dependencies, and other planning information, used to produce a project schedule along with other scheduling artifacts.

---

*Define:* **Schedule Network Analysis**

A technique to identify early and late start dates, as well as early and late finish dates, for the uncompleted portions of project activities.

---

*Define:* **Schedule Performance Index (SPI)**

A measure of schedule efficiency expressed as the ratio of earned value to planned value.

---

# Definitions

*Define:* **Schedule Variance (SV)**

A measure of schedule performance expressed as the difference between the earned value and the planned value.

*Define:* **Scheduling Tool**

A tool that provides schedule component names, definitions, structural relationships, and formats that support the application of a scheduling method.

*Define:* **Scope**

The sum of the products, services and results to be provided as a project. See also project scope and product scope.

*Define:* **Scope Baseline**

The approved version of a scope statement work breakdown structure (WBS), and its associated WBS dictionary, that can be changed using formal change control procedures and is used as a basis for comparison to actual results.

*Define:* **Scope Creep**

The uncontrolled expansion to product or project scope without adjustments to time, cost and resources.

*Define:* **Scope Management Plan**

A component of the project management plan that describes how the scope will be defined developed, monitored, controlled, and validated.

*Define:* **Secondary Risk**

A risk that arises as a direct result of implementing a risk response.

*Define:* **Self-Organizing Teams**

A team formation where the team functions with an absence of centralized control.

*Define:* **Seller**

A provider or supplier of products, services, or results to an organization.

*Define:* **Seller Proposals**

Formal responses from sellers to a request for proposal or other procurement document specifying the price, commercial terms of sale, and technical specifications or capabilities the seller will do for the requesting organization that, if accepted, would bind the seller to perform the resulting agreement.

*Define:* **Sensitivity Analysis**

An analysis technique to determine which individual project risks or other sources of uncertainty have the most potential impact on project outcomes, by correlating variations in project outcomes with variations in elements of a quantitative risk analysis model.

*Define:* **Sequence Activities**

The process of identifying and documenting relationships among the project activities.

# Definitions

*Define:* **Service Level Agreement (SLA)**

A contract between a service provider (either internal or external) and the end user that defines the level of service expected from the service provider.

---

*Define:* **Simulation**

An analytical technique that models the combined effect of uncertainties to evaluate their potential impact on objectives.

---

*Define:* **Source Selection Criteria**

A set of attributes desired by the buyer which a seller is required to meet or exceed to be selected for a contract.

---

*Define:* **Specification**

A precise statement of the needs to be satisfied and the essential characteristics that are required.

---

*Define:* **Specification Limits**

The area, on either side of the centerline, or mean, of data plotted on a control chart that meets the customer's requirements for a product or service. This area may be greater than or less than the area defined by the control limits. See also control limits.

---

*Define:* **Sponsor**

A person or group who provides resources and support for the project, program, or portfolio and is accountable for enabling success.

---

*Define:* **Sponsoring Organization**

The entity responsible for providing the project's sponsor and a conduit for project funding or other project resources.

---

*Define:* **Stakeholder**

An individual, group, or organization that may affect, be affected by, or perceive itself to be affected by a decision, activity, or outcome of a project, program, or portfolio.

---

*Define:* **Stakeholder Analysis**

A technique of systematically gathering and analyzing quantitative and qualitative information to determine whose interests should be considered throughout the project.

---

*Define:* **Stakeholder Engagement Assessment Matrix**

A matrix that compares current and desired stakeholder engagement levels.

---

*Define:* **Stakeholder Engagement Plan**

A component of the project management plan that identifies the strategies and actions required to promote productive involvement of stakeholders in project or program decision making and execution.

---

*Define:* **Stakeholder Register**

A project document including the identification, assessment, and classification of project stakeholders.

# Definitions

*Define:* **Standard**

A document established by an authority, custom, or general consent as a model or example.

*Define:* **Start Date**

A point in time associated with a schedule activity's start, usually qualified by one of the following: actual, planned, estimated, scheduled, early, late, target. baseline, or current.

*Define:* **Start-to-Finish (SF)**

A logical relationship in which a successor activity cannot finish until a predecessor activity has started.

*Define:* **Start-to-Start (SS)**

A logical relationship in which a successor activity cannot start until a predecessor activity has started.

*Define:* **Statement of Work (SOW)**

A narrative description of products, services, or results to be delivered by the project.

*Define:* **Statistical Sampling**

Choosing part of a population of interest for inspection.

*Define:* **Successor Activity**

A dependent activity that logically comes after another activity in a schedule.

*Define:* **Summary Activity**

A group of related schedule activities aggregated and displayed as a single activity.

*Define:* **SWOT Analysis**

Analysis of strengths, weaknesses, opportunities, and threats of an organization, project, or option.

*Define:* **Tacit Knowledge**

Personal knowledge that can be difficult to articulate and share such as beliefs, experience, and insights.

*Define:* **Tailoring**

Determining the appropriate combination of processes, inputs, tools, techniques, outputs, and life cycle phases to manage a project.

*Define:* **Team Charter**

A document that records the team values, agreements, and operating guidelines, as well as establishing clear expectations regarding acceptable behavior by project team members.

*Define:* **Team Management Plan**

A component of the resource management plan that describes when and how new team members will be acquired and how long they will be needed.

# Definitions

*Define:* **Technique**

A defined systematic procedure employed by a human resource to perform an activity to produce a product or result or deliver a service, and that may employ one or more tools.

*Define:* **Templates**

A partially complete document in a predefined format that provides a defined structure for collecting, organizing, and presenting information and data.

*Define:* **Test and Evaluation Documents**

Project documents that describe the activities used to determine if the product meets the quality objectives stated in the quality management plan.

*Define:* **Threat**

A risk that would have a negative effect on one or more project objectives.

*Define:* **Three-Point Estimating**

A technique used to estimate cost or duration by applying an average or weighted average of optimistic, pessimistic, and most likely estimates when there is uncertainty with the individual activity estimates.

*Define:* **Threshold**

A predetermined value of a measurable project variable that represents a limit that requires action to be taken if it is reached.

*Define:* **Time and Material Contract (T&M)**

A type of contract that is a hybrid contractual arrangement containing aspects of both cost-reimbursable and fixed-price contracts.

*Define:* **To-Complete Performance Index (TCPI)**

A measure of the cost performance that is required to be achieved with the remaining resources in order to meet a specified management goal, expressed as the ratio of the cost to finish the outstanding work to the remaining budget.

*Define:* **Tolerance**

The quantified description of acceptable variation for a quality requirement.

*Define:* **Tool**

Something tangible, such as a template or software program, used in performing an activity to produce a product or result.

*Define:* **Tornado Diagram**

A special type of bar chart used in sensitivity analysis for comparing the relative importance of the variables.

*Define:* **Total Float**

The amount of time that a schedule activity can be delayed or extended from its early start date without delaying the project finish date or violating a schedule constraint.

# Definitions

*Define:* **Trend Analysis**

An analytical technique that uses mathematical models to forecast future outcomes based on historical results.

---

*Define:* **Trigger Condition**

An event or situation that indicates that a risk is about to occur.

---

*Define:* **Unanimity**

Agreement by everyone in the group on a single course of action.

---

*Define:* **Update**

A modification to any deliverable, project management plan component, or project document that is not under formal change control.

---

*Define:* **Validate Scope**

The process of formalizing acceptance of the completed project deliverables.

---

*Define:* **Validation**

The assurance that a product, service, or result meets the needs of the customer and other identified stakeholders. Contrast with verification.

---

*Define:* **Variance**

A quantifiable deviation, departure, or divergence away from a known baseline or expected value.

---

*Define:* **Variance Analysis**

A technique for determining the cause and degree of difference between the baseline and actual performance.

---

*Define:* **Variance at Completion (VAC)**

A projection of the amount of budget deficit or surplus, expressed as the difference between the budget at completion and the estimate at completion.

---

*Define:* **Variation**

An actual condition that is different from the expected condition that is contained in the baseline plan.

---

*Define:* **Verification**

The evaluation of whether or not a product, service, or result complies with a regulation, requirement, specification, or imposed condition. Contrast with validation.

---

*Define:* **Verified Deliverables**

Completed project deliverables that have been checked and confirmed for correctness through the Control Quality process.

---

*Define:* **Virtual Teams**

Groups of people with a shared goal who fulfill their roles with little or no time spent meeting face to face.

---

# Definitions

*Define:* **Voice of the Customer**

A planning technique used to provide products, services, and results that truly reflect customer requirements by translating those customer requirements into the appropriate technical requirements for each phase of project product development.

*Define:* **WBS Dictionary**

A document that provides detailed deliverable, activity and scheduling information about each component in the work breakdown structure.

*Define:* **What-If Scenario Analysis**

The process of evaluating scenarios in order to predict their effect on project objectives.

*Define:* **Work Breakdown Structure (WBS)**

A hierarchical decomposition of the total scope of work to be carried out by the project team to accomplish the project objectives and create the required deliverables.

*Define:* **Work Breakdown Structure Component**

An entry in the work breakdown structure that can be at any level.

*Define:* **Work Package**

The work defined at the lowest level of the work breakdown structure for which cost and duration are estimated and managed.

*Define:* **Work Performance Data**

The raw observations and measurements identified during activities being performed to carry out the project work.

*Define:* **Work Performance Information**

The performance data collected from controlling processes, analyzed in comparison with project management plan components, project documents, and other work performance information.

*Define:* **Work Performance Reports**

The physical or electronic representation of work performance information compiled in project documents Intended to generate decisions, actions, or awareness.

Printed in Great Britain
by Amazon